# COMMON MISTAKES
# PARENTS
## make about their
# CHILDREN

WITH TIPS FOR PARENTING

FATAI KASALI

COMMON MISTAKES PARENTS MAKE ABOUT THEIR CHILDREN

Copyright © 2017 Fatai Kasali

The author has asserted his right to be identified as the author of this work in accordance with the Copyright, Designs and Patents Act 1988.

All rights reserved. No part of this publication may be reproduced, stored in a retrieval system, or transmitted, in any form or by any means, electronic, mechanical, photocopying, recording or otherwise without the prior permission of the author.

All Scripture quotations, unless otherwise indicated, are taken from the Holy Bible, King James Version, Cambridge University Press, Oxford University Press, Harper Collins and the Queen's Printers.

Published in the United Kingdom by Glory Publishing.

ISBN: 978-0-9926138-8-4

# ACKNOWLEDGEMENTS

I give the almighty God all the glory for the grace to write this book. I thank Him for His gifts that have enabled me to complete it. Blessed be His holy name.

I would like to acknowledge the immense contribution of my wife, Felicia Ebunlomo, towards the writing of this book. My two sons, Daniel and David, have also been very supportive.

To all those who have contributed in one way or another to the beauty of this work, thank you very much. May God Almighty bless you all.

# INTRODUCTION

Parenting is the act of taking the role of a parent in the life of a child. It includes watching over and giving care to a child for his or her upbringing and development – spiritually, physically, mentally and morally. It also includes provision for the child's needs. The tasks involved in parenting clearly require maturity and knowledge on the part of the parents.

This book explains that parenting can't be effective in the absence of certain factors, such as a conducive environment and love. You will learn in this book that; the kind of atmosphere at home affects how children will react to training from their parents.

Children are God-given. Therefore, children should be brought up in life using God as a model. God is love and He is also a Father. For effective parenting, it is wise to study how God relates to His children. This is explored in this book.

Similarly, I explore what the Bible says about the seed of the righteous. This is to reveal the mind of God as regards children. With such understanding, parents can pray into the lives of their children; what has been written about them. Therefore, this book ends with some prayer points that could be used by parents.

I pray that as you use this book, the mind of God will manifest in the lives of your children. Amen

# CONTENTS

1    The role of parents in the home . . . . . . . . . . . . . . . . . . . 9
2    Fundamental truths about children . . . . . . . . . . . . . . . . 19
3    Parenting – get it right . . . . . . . . . . . . . . . . . . . . . . . . . 33
4    Common mistakes parents make about their children . . 51
5    Parenting by love . . . . . . . . . . . . . . . . . . . . . . . . . . . . . 65
6    Counsel from the scriptures . . . . . . . . . . . . . . . . . . . . . 73
7    The seed of the righteous . . . . . . . . . . . . . . . . . . . . . . . 87

One

# THE ROLE OF PARENTS IN THE HOME

A home is a place where family dwells. It comprises parents and their children.

It is important for parents to understand the meaning of a home, as this will determine their roles. It will also help the parents to understand whether or not they have made their home a real home.

In the Bible, LUKE 15:11-32 tells the story of a prodigal son who left his home for a foreign land. Unfortunately, he could not find a home in that foreign land until he returned to his real home. He only found a house in a foreign land – not a home.

A home can be described as follows:

## 1. A place of love

It is a place where members of the family find affection, care and security. If your home cannot provide this for them, it is not yet a home.

## 2. A place of permanent membership

Irrespective of distance, you can never be separated from your home, if it is a true home. You have not seen your home as a home if you have considered divorcing your spouse and moving out of the home. In reality, there is nothing that can replace your home.

## 3. A place that has no price

You can place a price on a house not a home. You can buy a house, but you can't buy a home. A house is a building, but a home is family living together.

If your home members (children and spouse) are not valuable to you or you don't treat them as important, you don't know your home as a home. In a home, every member is valuable because they are irreplaceable.

## 4. A place where members can never be strangers

If you are treating your spouse or children as strangers at home, you have no understanding of a home. At home, every member should be free. Home is the only place where members feel welcome and not as stranger. A home must be welcoming to every member.

## 5. A place where a genuine sense of belonging is found

A home is a place you have a real sense of belonging. Every member believes they are part of the home. You are a part of your home by natural, not by human selection. If you still feel as if there is a better place where you belong, you have not considered your home a home. There should never be any other place that is like a home to you.

## 6. A place of foundation for an individual

Your home is your origin and source. It is the place where you are formed. Therefore, parents must be careful about their children's development, especially in terms of character development and the kind of things parents expose their children to at home.

## 7. A place where the heart dwells

Under a normal situation, wherever you go, you will always think of home – your children and spouse. For example, if your heart is not focusing on your home irrespective of where you are at any particular time, then, you have not seen your home as home.

## 8. A place that has no equal

There should be no place like home. If you see another place better than your home, then you have not regarded your home as your home.

## 9. A place that holds records and vital information about an individual

At home, your secrets can be found. Home holds vital information about you and every other member. That is why parents must not allow just anybody to come and dwell with them in their home, because they will have access to secrets of the family.

## 10. A place of resuscitation

When people become tired and weak, they return home for resuscitation. Your home is not a home if members can't find strength, hope, joy, encouragement and renewal there.

## 11. A place of preparation

Life starts from home. Who your child will become in future starts from home. That is why parents must be careful how members of their home grow up in life.

## 12. A place where a name is given

Every child receives a name from home. Also, a child will be described by the society based on how he or she was developed at home.

## JOINT RESPONSIBILITIES OF HUSBAND AND WIFE AT HOME

### 1. They must be a 'helpmate' to each other

This means they must help each other to live a fulfilling life.

*Two are better than one; because they have a good reward for their labour. For if they fall, the one will lift up his fellow: but woe to him that is alone when he falleth; for he hath not another to help him up. Again, if two lie together, then they have heat: but how can one be warm alone? And if one prevail against him, two shall withstand him; and a threefold cord is not quickly broken.* ECCLESIASTES 4:9-12.

In other words, couples are designed to help each other to overcome the challenges of life. For example, in parenting, they must work together. The one that is good at parenting must help the other to become better in parenting. Parenting must not be left to one parent only. It should be the joint responsibility of both parents.

### 2. They must practice mutual submission to each other

*Submitting yourselves one to another in the fear of God.*
EPHESIANS 5:21

That is, a couple must obey each other in the fear of God. They must practise this in parenting. They must not enter into arguments in front of their children, so as not to be a bad example to them. They must submit to each other's opinion in the presence of their children, and discuss any differences of opinion away from their children.

### 3. They must enforce obedience to God at home

They must jointly ensure that every member of the family serves God.

For example, in ACTS 10:1-2, Cornelius enforced religion in his home: There was a certain man in Caesarea called Cornelius, a centurion of the band called the Italian band, a devout man, and one that feared God with all his house, which gave much alms to the people, and prayed to God alway.

He served God with his entire household (that means, everybody who lived at his home). It is the joint responsibility of the parents to ensure that every member of their home obeys and serves God.

Similarly, in Acts 16, Lydia enforced religion in her home: And when she was baptized, and her household, she besought us, saying, If ye have judged me to be faithful to the Lord, come into my house, and abide there. And she constrained us.

She ensured that every member of her home got baptised. She made her home members do as she had done. Similarly, teach your children to follow you in serving God. There will come a time when they have to choose whether to serve God or not for themselves, but until then, God expects you to lead them in obedience to Him.

## 4. They must nurture their children

Both parents must care for their children, educate them and raise them up in life.

In 1 Samuel 1:22-24, Hannah and her husband raised Samuel up before it was time for him to be given unto the Lord. It is the joint responsibility of both parents to nurture their children.

## 5. They must be good examples to their children

For example, their children must emulate them in:

- A - **Faith.** Timothy emulated the faith of his mother and grandmother.

    *When I call to remembrance the unfeigned faith that is in thee, which dwelt first in thy grandmother Lois, and thy mother Eunice; and I am persuaded that in thee also.* 2 Timothy 1:5.

- B - **Serving God.** Jehoshaphat emulated his father in his service to God.

*And the LORD was with Jehoshaphat, because he walked in the first ways of his father David, and sought not unto Baalim...* 2 CHRONICLES 17:3.

C - **Godly character.** As a parent, your children must learn from you how good Christians talk to people, treat people, practise a spirit-filled and controlled life and a life of holiness—a life without spot.

*Let no man despise thy youth; but be thou an example of the believers, in word, in conversation, in charity, in spirit, in faith, in purity.* 1 TIMOTHY 4:12.

## 6. They must create an atmosphere at home that is conducive for bringing up good children

Examples of the right atmosphere include:

A - **An atmosphere of love.** A child brought up in love will show love outside the home and grow up emotionally matured.

*That they may teach the young women to be sober, to love their husbands, to love their children.* TITUS 2:4.

B - **An atmosphere of mercy.** For example, in Jesus' parable the prodigal son decided to return home because he knew he would find mercy there:

*I will arise and go to my father, and will say unto him, Father, I have sinned against heaven, and before thee...* LUKE 15:18.

For a prodigal son to think of coming back home, both parents must be people of love and mercy. A home filled with mercy will encourage a child who sins to confess and repent. A child will be afraid of confession if he or she knows that there is no possibility of mercy and forgiveness at home. Such a child will be tempted to hide his or her sin.

*But if any widow have children or nephews, let them learn first to shew piety at home, and to requite their parents: for that is good and acceptable before God.* 1 TIMOTHY 5:4.

C - **An atmosphere of learning.** Home should be a place where members can learn.

*And she had a sister called Mary, which also sat at Jesus' feet, and heard his word.* LUKE 10:39.

Mary could sit down to learn at Jesus' feet because the atmosphere at home permitted it. For example, if all the members were busy fighting when Jesus came, learning would have been impossible. It is only a peaceful home that can promote learning.

## 7. They must show unforgettable love to their children

*Can a woman forget her sucking child, that she should not have compassion on the son of her womb? Yea, they may forget, yet will I not forget thee.* ISAIAH 49:15.

The love that a genuine mother shows to her child is unforgettable. This will follow the child even when he/she grows up. A child who has experienced unforgettable love at home will always remember that home wherever he or she goes in life.

*And when he came to himself, he said, How many hired servants of my father's have bread enough and to spare, and I perish with hunger!* LUKE 15:17.

When life in a foreign land became very hard for the prodigal son, he was still able to remember the love of his father. It is an unforgettable love.

Parents must love their children in such a way that they will find it hard to forget for the rest of their lives. Such love makes an indelible mark on the heart.

## 8. They must intercede continually for their children

Abraham interceded for his son:

*And Abraham said unto God, O that Ishmael might live before thee!* GENESIS 17:18.

A Syrophenician woman interceded for her child:

*The woman was a Greek, a Syrophenician by nation; and she besought him that he would cast forth the devil out of her daughter* MARK 7:26.

A father interceded for his daughter:

*And besought him greatly, saying, My little daughter lieth at the point of death: I pray thee, come and lay thy hands on her, that she may be healed; and she shall live.* MARK 5:23.

In a Christian home, both parents must continually seek the face of God for their children. Pray for your children always.

## 9. They must seek God's guidance regarding their children

*Then Manoah intreated the LORD, and said, O my Lord, let the man of God which thou didst send come again unto us, and teach us what we shall do unto the child that shall be born.* JUDGES 13:8.

In this story, the parents of Samson sought the face of God for guidance about how to raise him. Similarly, you must ask God about His plan and destiny for your children. Ask God how to bring up your children.

## 10. They must provide for their home

*Behold, the third time I am ready to come to you; and I will not be burdensome to you: for I seek not yours but you: for the children ought not to lay up for the parents, but the parents for the children.* 2 CORINTHIANS 12:14.

It is the joint responsibility of both parents to provide for their home, and it's not just about finances – but providing for their children's emotional and social needs, academic support, etc.

## 11. They must always bless their home

Parents must regularly invoke blessings on their home.

*And all the people departed every man to his house: and David returned to bless his house.* 1 Chronicles 16:43.

Here; the Bible says that David blessed his home. Both parents must speak good words into their home and declare the blessings of God on their family.

## 12. They must train up their children

*Train up a child in the way he should go: and when he is old, he will not depart from it.* Proverbs 22:6.

Both parents must have an agreed plan and way of training their children in how to live for God. Such training involves personal teaching and guidance, but it could also involve formal or informal education.

## Two

# FUNDAMENTAL TRUTHS ABOUT CHILDREN

As parents, you must understand certain facts about children so you will know the best methods to adopt in dealing with them.

The following truths are fundamental about children and should be used as a guide in all your dealings with them.

### 1. Children are a heritage from the Lord

*Lo, children are an heritage of the LORD: and the fruit of the womb is his reward.* PSALM 127:3.

Heritage is something that is passed to somebody from the previous generation or generations. It is an inheritance.

This implies that you are not the original owner of those children. God is the original owner. They were given to you by God. Before you gave birth to them, those children were existing in God and God later chose to pass them to you to own as an inheritance.

But it should be noted that:

- A - **Inheritance comes with responsibility.** It is your responsibility to manage them well. If you manage your children well, they will become a blessing to you in all your days.

B - **Inheritance comes with accountability.** One day, you will give an account to God about how you have managed your children. Many parents are already under the judgement of God because they messed up the children God gave them.

## 2. Children are like angels in your house

They may not always act like it, but your little children are like angels in the house!

*Out of the mouth of babes and sucklings hast thou ordained strength because of thine enemies, that thou mightest still the enemy and the avenger.* PSALM 8:2.

This verse states that God has ordained praise out of the mouths of little children. Angels praise God continually in heaven. Probably due to the purity of their hearts, children are compared with angels. Furthermore, if children can be compared with angels, it implies that they can do certain things angels do. For example:

A - **Children can bless as angels can.** *Her children arise up, and call her blessed; her husband also, and he praiseth her.* PROVERBS 31:28.

This verse indicates that a virtuous woman will attract blessings from her children. They will bless her because of the care they receive from her. This implies that if you care for your children very well, there are certain blessings that God will be sending into your life. When your children pray for you, God will hear in heaven.

For example, a Christian brother had been seeking a job without success but one day, during a family prayer time, his four-year-old child prayed that God would provide a job for his dad. The dad got a job that week. God listens to children.

B - **Children can curse as angels can.** In their innocence, if your children speak a word of curse about you, it may rest, especially if there is a genuine ground for it. A parent that continually abuses his or her child will enter into spiritual problems if that child should place a curse on him or her. When your child makes a genuine cry to heaven, God will respond accordingly.

C - **Children are agents of light as angels are.** A parent who can pay close attention to his or her children will discover that God speaks through children.

*At that time Jesus answered and said, I thank thee, O Father, Lord of heaven and earth, because thou hast hid these things from the wise and prudent, and hast revealed them unto babes.* MATTHEW 11:25.

Due to their innocence, God sometimes finds it easier to speak through children.

In 1 SAMUEL 3, God spoke through a young boy called Samuel even though the elderly priest Eli was still alive.

This could be due to the fact that the hearts of children are pure, and they are malleable. This makes it easy for them to attract the light of God in terms of revelation. In many situations, God may speak to you through your children.

D - **Children offer protection as angels do.** Due to the presence of children in your house, there are certain evils you will escape. God always give special consideration to places and homes where there are children. This is because children are vulnerable and God will always give special consideration to the vulnerable. As a parent, if you are wise enough to take care of your children, you will enjoy certain privileges from God. The presence of children around you will bring you certain opportunities from God.

## 3. Children are innocent in all their ways

That is, children are naïve, inexperienced and not intentionally harmful. In many situations, children don't know what they are doing, nor do they know the implications of their actions. So, due to their innocence, the following precautions should be adhered to:

**A - Children should not be left alone.** *The rod and reproof give wisdom: but a child left to himself bringeth his mother to shame.* PROVERBS 29:15.

That is, you must always be available to guide and tutor your children.

*Now I say, that the heir, as long as he is a child, differeth nothing from a servant, though he be lord of all; but is under tutors and governors until the time appointed of the father.* GALATIANS 4:1-2.

This verse indicates that your children must be under your tutorship until they come of age. You must always guide and direct your children till they grow up to become an adult. It is your responsibility to have time for your children's upbringing and to discipline them. Unfortunately, many parents have no time for their children, due to the excuse of commitments at work. Don't let the devil use your job to keep you away from your children, or he may take over their lives. A child left to him or herself is easy prey for the devil.

**B - Children deserve pity.** It is a common belief that a person who lacks enough mental capacity to understand the implication of his or her actions deserves pity. This is why someone with mental problems who commits a crime is often dealt with leniently on the grounds of 'diminished responsibility'. It follows that, as a parent, you must always be merciful and compassionate to your children too, as their minds are not fully developed.

*Like as a father pitieth his children, so the LORD pitieth them that fear him.* PSALM 103:13.

You must show pity to your children as God does towards you as His child.

You must know that God pities us because in many situations we don't really understand the full implications of some of our actions. In many situations, if we did understand how our actions would affect others or influence events, we would not do many of the things that we do. Therefore, God has chosen to continually show you mercy and compassion, understanding that you are just a little child in His hands. Therefore, you must show the same understanding towards your children.

*Nevertheless they did flatter him with their mouth, and they lied unto him with their tongues. For their heart was not right with him, neither were they stedfast in his covenant. But he, being full of compassion, forgave their iniquity, and destroyed them not: yea, many a time turned he his anger away, and did not stir up all his wrath. For he remembered that they were but flesh; a wind that passeth away, and cometh not again.* PSALM 78:36-39.

This psalm tells us how God treats us as His children. He is full of compassion. Therefore, you must be a merciful parent to your children. You must avoid being excessively harsh and rigid in your treatment of them.

## 4. Your children are sanctified

Because you are a Christian, all your children are sanctified by the Lord.

*For the unbelieving husband is sanctified by the wife, and the unbelieving wife is sanctified by the husband: else were your children unclean; but now are they holy.* 1 CORINTHIANS 7:14.

To be sanctified means to be separated unto the Lord for His use. This is the root meaning of holiness – to be set apart for God.

You need to be aware that it is God's plan for the children He gives you to be brought to Him for His use. God wants to use your children for His own glory and the good of others.

*Then were there brought unto him little children, that he should put his hands on them, and pray: and the disciples rebuked them. But*

*Jesus said, Suffer little children, and forbid them not, to come unto me: for of such is the kingdom of heaven.* MATTHEW 19:13-14.

Here Matthew records how children were brought to Jesus for Him to bless them, but the disciples didn't think Jesus should be bothered with them. Jesus rebuked his disciples for hindering the children from coming to Him. This shows the importance God places on children. God wants your children to be brought to Him at an early age so that He can bless them and use them.

This means that God will count it as a sin if any parent prevents his or her children from coming to Him, especially at an early age.

It is important for you to know that God has already separated your children unto Himself before they were born, and His expectation is that you will bring them to Him for His use. This truth is revealed in Jeremiah 1, where God tells Jeremiah that He ordained him before he was formed in the womb of his mother. You must encourage your children to walk in the sanctification that God has provided for them. Encourage your children to attend church services and serve God from an early age.

## 5. Children are imitators

An imitator is someone who copies the words or behaviour of another person. Children always want to be what they see or hear.

For example, Timothy saw faith in his mother and grandmother and he imitated it:

*When I call to remembrance the unfeigned faith that is in thee, which dwelt first in thy grandmother Lois, and thy mother Eunice; and I am persuaded that in thee also.* 2 TIMOTHY 1:5.

Conversely, if Timothy, while growing up, saw his parents practising evil, he would be likely to imitate that instead.

This is the reason why, as a parent, you must be careful what your children hear or see through you. Be careful how you speak and act in front of them.

Because Parents are the first point of contact children have as they enter into this world, so children tend to imitate their parents more than anyone else. This begins to change when they reach their teenage years and become more influenced by their peers and other people they encounter, which is why it is vital to set them a good example whilst they are influenced by you.

If you set a bad example, they will imitate that. For example, a boy may abuse women when he becomes an adult because he grew up seeing his father treating his mother badly.

It is important for you to know that your children will copy your habits, whether good or bad, and in the very near future, they will put them into practice. It is my prayer that you will be a good example to your children, in Jesus' name. Amen

## 6. Your children are for your imitation

You might not realise that God gives you children so that you can learn from them. There are a lot of lessons your children can teach you.

*Verily I say unto you, except ye be converted, and become as little children, ye shall not enter into the kingdom of heaven. Whosoever therefore shall humble himself as this little child, the same is greatest in the kingdom of heaven.* MATTHEW 18:3-4.

God expects you to practise a child-like faith. Close examination of the best traits of children will reveal that they are believing, trusting and accepting. They can also be humble, obedient, submissive, forgiving to each other, manageable and teachable – just as in the list of the fruit of the Spirit detailed in GALATIANS 5. All these are the values of the kingdom of God.

Therefore, if you can play close attention to your children as they relate to others, you will be reminding yourself constantly of the godly character God expects from you.

## 7. Children are easy to destroy but not easy to repair

It is very important for you to understand the vulnerability of children. They are not strong enough to withstand emotional torture and stress. You are destroying your children emotionally if you are always rebuking them unreasonably, or being unjustifiably angry towards them.

You need to understand that your angry look and appearance to your children is having a negative emotional impact on them. A child who is continually subjected to abuse will become damaged emotionally, and once grown up with that damage, it will be difficult to cure. Similarly, you must be aware that once a child develops negative opinions about his or her parents, it will be difficult to change those views.

Experience shows these things to be true, but the Bible also warns us about this. COLOSSIANS 3:21 says: *Fathers, provoke not your children to anger, lest they be discouraged.* This implies that provocation can take away the courage of a child. That in turn leads to many other problems, such as low self-esteem and a bad temperament.

You must avoid provoking your children. Children become resentful and develop a wrong mind-set if they have a bitter experience of their parents. There are many parents who have lost the respect of their children because of the way in which they have treated their children.

## 8. The future of your children could be moulded by your words

In your relationship with your children, you must understand that your words matter. Therefore, you must be mindful of what passes your lips when you are speaking to your children or speaking about them.

As a parent, you have a spiritual authority over your children, especially when they are still young. The kind of words you speak into their lives will mould their mind, thinking system and even their destiny. There are many children that have lost self-esteem because of wrong words their parents spoke to them when growing up.

*And Jabez was more honourable than his brethren: and his mother called his name Jabez, saying, Because I bare him with sorrow.*
1 CHRONICLES 4:9.

In this Bible story, the mother of Jabez named him after the sorrowful event she passed through during her delivery of Jabez. This served as a constant reminder every time someone called his name, is bound to have affected him spiritually. It is very likely that Jabez always had in mind the pain his mother passed through in order to give him birth. Jabez's imagination and expectations were no doubt filled with sorrow, and his life may well have been controlled by the spirit of sorrow his mother unknowingly attached to the destiny of Jabez.

That said, the Bible says that Jabez was honourable and his requests to God were answered (1 CHRONICLES 4:9-10), so, we can always have hope that the worst of childhood experiences can be overcome with faith. But how much better would his life have been without such a distressing start?

Your words matter in the life of your children. The perceptions, emotions and ideas you continually speak into the lives of your children may determine their future.

## 9. Children are naturally inquisitive

Children are always wanting to know about something. They like asking questions. This helps to shape their thinking and knowledge. You must be aware that as your children ask you questions and you give them answers, you are indirectly moulding their mind. Therefore, as a parent, you must be careful how you answer your children, because your answers will affect your children's development.

Due to their innocence, children are quick to believe and accept whatever they hear, especially from their parents. Consequently, their mind will function in a certain way.

In EXODUS 12:26-27, God told the Israelites to answer their children correctly when they ask questions about the Passover. This implies that God was preparing the minds of the young Israelites for what would happen to them in the future. God wanted the children to remember what he had done for them through Moses, so that they would have faith in him in the future. So when children ask questions, parents must tell the truth. The truth must be given to them in an age-appropriate way, but not avoided.

It is also advisable for parents to encourage their children to be inquisitive. As a parent, you must encourage them to ask you questions because it is a way of educating them and empowering their minds to develop. But you must give an honest answer to their questions.

If you don't know a particular answer to a question, you must be courageous enough to tell the truth. But don't leave it there. It is important that after telling your children that you don't know the answer, you tell them that you will find out the answer and get back to them. Don't forget to fulfil this promise, or you will disappoint them. Failing to keep your promises makes them feel you don't care about them. You must never leave your children in limbo (the condition of prolonged uncertainty).

If you ignore your children's questions, you are denying their minds the chance to develop, and if you give them the wrong answer and they find out later, you will lose their respect and trust, and confuse them.

## 10. Children will always need their parent's understanding

It is imperative to note that children and adults are totally different in many ways. Children are not mini-adults. For example, children are different in terms of experience, knowledge, understanding and physique. Parents must deal with their children with the understanding that they are not dealing with adults. Therefore, parents must adjust their expectations accordingly. Never expect from a child, what you would expect from an adult.

*But when that which is perfect is come, then that which is in part shall be done away. When I was a child, I spake as a child, I understood as a child, I thought as a child: but when I became a man, I put away childish things.* 1 Corinthians 13:10-11.

This verse indicates that there is a way children speak, understand and think that is unique to children. Until a child grows to be an adult, the way he or she speaks, understands and thinks will remain childlike (though some mature more quickly than others). Therefore, you need to be realistic when dealing with your children, otherwise you will always experience disappointment and frustration.

## 11. God has incorporated your children into his plans for your life

As a parent, you must know that whatever God wills for your life, your children are always part of His plans. The promises of God for your life take your children into consideration.

*For the promise is unto you, and to your children, and to all that are afar off, even as many as the Lord our God shall call.* Acts 2:39.

The promise shows that God had your children in mind when He was designing your life. His promises for your life will never exclude your children. His blessings for your life will always take into consideration your children. Therefore, it is an error on your part if you prevent your children from enjoying the blessings God gives you. Similarly, it's wrong for you to draw closer to God while leaving your children far away from Him.

God told the Israelites in Deuteronomy 11:19 to teach their children His laws so that they could obey God just as their parents did. When God says that you must be holy, He expects the same standard from your children.

## 12. Children are affected by the signs of the end time

Humanity is now living in the end times – the last age, during which the second coming of Jesus Christ will take place. As a result, every human being, both young and old, will be affected by the signs of the end times.

*And the brother shall deliver up the brother to death, and the father the child: and the children shall rise up against their parents, and cause them to be put to death.* MATTHEW 10:21.

Jesus reveals that children will be caught up in the troubles of the end times. They will become more rebellious. Therefore, parents must be alert, watching out for any manifestations of the signs of the times in their children, and deal with them urgently. Keep a close eye on your children, to see if they are rebelling against you in any way.

*There is a generation that curseth their father, and doth not bless their mother.* PROVERBS 30:11.

This generation is already here, as we await the second coming of Jesus Christ. Children are going to become more and more disobedient and defiant. Rebellious children don't obey their parents' instructions and don't respect them. In these end times, Satan is seriously contending for the lives of children, exploiting their vulnerability. But as a parent, you can frustrate all these negative influences in the lives of your children by dealing with them early and applying proper biblical parenting standards.

So, if you notice any sign of rebellion in your children, deal with it quickly, prayerfully and wisely.

## 13. Children are highly esteemed in God's kingdom

*But Jesus said, Suffer little children, and forbid them not, to come unto me: for of such is the kingdom of heaven.* MATTHEW 19:14.

This means that children occupy a very significant position in the kingdom of God. Therefore, as a parent, you must place your children in an important position in your life. Whatever that is important to you will receive your special care and attention. You must treat your children in the same manner.

## 14. God is their defence

It is a great mistake to think that children are helpless and that you can treat them as you like.

God is a God of the weak and vulnerable. He will arise to defend the helpless that have nobody to defend them – and that includes your children.

*Leave thy fatherless children, I will preserve them alive; and let thy widows trust in me.* JEREMIAH 49:11.

God says He will take care of children who have nobody to take care of them.

*He doth execute the judgment of the fatherless and widow, and loveth the stranger, in giving him food and raiment.* DEUTERONOMY 10:18.

God says He will maintain justice in the affairs of helpless children. He will judge their oppressors.

*Remove not the old landmark; and enter not into the fields of the fatherless: For their redeemer is mighty; he shall plead their cause with thee.* PROVERBS 23:10-11.

God says He is a mighty God who will defend the cause of helpless children. God will always defend the weak and vulnerable. For example, there are many parents who are under the judgement of God today because of the way they mistreated their children. Therefore, if you don't want to invite the wrath of God, never maltreat your children. If their cry reaches heaven, you will find yourself in a difficult situation before God. It is my prayer that you will not be found guilty over the affairs of your children, in Jesus' name. Amen

Three

# PARENTING – GET IT RIGHT

Parenting is not fathering a child or giving birth to a child – it is the act of giving ongoing care, provision and protection for all a child's life. You are responsible for the spiritual, physical, mental and moral development of your children.

PROVERBS 22:6 says: *Train up a child in the way he should go: and when he is old, he will not depart from it.*

This implies that parenting is setting a child on a path for life's journey. As you parent a child, you are moulding him or her for the path he or she will choose in life.

Parenting is about training, and for this to be effective there are six questions that must be adequately answered. Right answers to these questions will enable you to get parenting right.

## 1. What are the objectives of training up a child?

That is, what do we intend to achieve when we train up a child?

The probable answers will include:

> A - **To help the child to form character.** Parents are to train their children to develop good character, because a child that

lacks good character is useless to God, man and himself or herself. Parents must understand that the future of a child depends on the character.

Character is not the same as personality. It is about the values that someone lives by, and whether they live up to those standards. It's about good qualities like resilience, determination, consistency, faithfulness and integrity.

In 1 SAMUEL 2:12, the sons of Eli are described as the sons of Belial. This means that they were useless, worthless and not profitable to anybody. God later destroyed them; after all, they were not usable by God due to their evil ways and lack of moral standards in the eyes of God.

A child that is deficient in the acceptable moral standards of a society will be treated as an outcast by society, and will not be considered for participation in anything worthwhile.

Considering the importance of good character, it is therefore very unfortunate if a parent neglects this vital truth in training up a child.

For example, some parents teach their children to fight back and get revenge when their friends wrong them. Such parents are indirectly training up their children to be aggressive, unforgiving and offence-controlled people. Children should be taught how to defend themselves but not to return evil for evil.

B - **To position the child to be used by God.** PSALM 127:3 says that children come from God. They are a heritage from Him. Consequently, EPHESIANS 6:4 declares that we should bring up our children in the *"nurture and admonition of the Lord"* or the training and instruction of God.

Considering that, it is not surprising that in 1 SAMUEL 1:28, Hannah chose to give her child (Samuel) to God for His use.

It is important to clarify that to be used by God does not mean that the child must be a full-time pastor, bishop, evangelist or prophet. But the child must grow up in a moral condition that will make him or her suitable for any assignment God gives. God needs human instruments He can use for good works such as helping the weak, blessing generations, touching lives positively and being agents of positive change in society.

It is vital to state that a child who is well morally-formed is much more useful to God for a glorious work than someone who is prey to temptation. God can use even the weakest of us for His glory, but nine times out of ten He will ignore those with the greater gifts if they do not have the moral character needed, and instead will choose the seemingly less talented. Why?

Because even the greatest of church leaders can fall from their position, and fail God, because of their moral weaknesses – bringing disrepute upon the Church. Therefore, adequate home training positions your child to be used by God for a good work that will last.

Incidentally, I would like to correct some wrong conceptions about training up a child that are practised in certain cultures. Some members of some communities consider training a child as an investment for their future. That is, they believe that they are training their children so that they can feed or care for them tomorrow. That is a selfish motive.

When you train up your child with a focus on making the child better morally, your attention will be on the child, not yourself. A well morally-formed child will definitely become a source of blessing to the parents, but that should not be the motivation for doing it. Therefore, as a parent, you don't focus on your selfish gain when you are bringing up your child. Your interest is to help the child to develop godly character for his or her own personal benefit and good, and for God's glory. If this is achieved, such a child will become grateful to you in future and be a blessing to you.

Considering the significance of child training, it is a wise thing for a parent to always ask himself or herself a question such as: "Can God use my child for a good purpose with the kind of training I am giving him/her?" If your answer is no, then you need to change your approach towards the kind of training you are giving your child.

## 2. What is a conducive atmosphere for training a child?

The answers include the following:

A - **Love.** Love is showing goodwill towards other people, regardless of how they treat us. And parental love is this agape kind of love – love without conditions. But in the context of family, love is not just an action but an emotion – we have a natural, God-given love for our children that drives us to care for them. But our human love is not enough. Parents can be exasperated by their children, and lose their temper. We need God's love when ours is inadequate for the task!

A loving attitude is essential for parenting. Love brings security, which is vital for children to flourish.

Training without love will breed a wrong interpretation in a child, even if the intention of the parent is good. Training giving in a context of harshness and inconsiderate behaviour will not be appreciated by a child. But a child who is trained in an atmosphere of love will feel secure in the hands of the parents, even if they punish him or her for the purpose of correction.

TITUS 2:4 admonishes parents to love their children. As a parent, create an atmosphere of love in your home so that your child can always find the love they need.

1 Peter 4:8 says that love covers up *"the multitude of sins"*. Parents must learn how to overlook offence, especially from their children. You must be 'thick skinned' – able to be loving even when your children are insolent. Correction for wrongdoing must be done out of love and not hatred.

While it is true that a child who does wrong should be corrected, it is also true that nobody is perfect. Therefore, your child always deserves another chance. When an error is committed, punishment may be required, but give your child another opportunity to prove how he or she can change from wrong behaviour. And don't give up, however many times they fail. This is true love. In every correction, it is the wrong behaviour you want to kill in the child, not the child himself or herself! This should be your guide: 'Do not crush the life out of your children because of error – give them room to grow.'

B - **Understanding.** In a home where there is understanding, men are treated as men and boys are treated as boys. The same applies to women and girls. The moral expectations must differ for young boys and girls. Do not treat a child like an adult. Do not expect from a child what only an adult can do or know. The wisdom of a young person differs from that of an adult.

A child needs training because he or she does not know certain things. Therefore, it is wrong for a parent to train a child as if the child has already been trained. Show understanding and sympathy. Your child is a child and not your spouse. Do not consider it a strange thing when your child makes a mistake. He or she is still growing in life, and part of growing up is learning from your mistakes.

C - **Liberty.** In an atmosphere of liberty, the individual is free to be natural. This helps parents to understand the real nature of their children. A child that is free will be allowed to make mistakes so that he or she can be corrected. When liberty is taken away from a child, such a child tends to pretend to be what he or she is not.

Create a home where there is freedom, allowing your child to be themselves. Don't impose your preferences on them, but encourage them to discover their own. (We are not talking about morals here, as we are all subject to God's standards. We are talking about preferences for such things as which sport they enjoy, which career they lean towards, which kind of music they like, what hobbies they enjoy, etc.)

Let your child act as him or herself and not like a clone of yourself or your spouse. And educate them about peer pressure, so that they are freed from the need to conform to someone else's expectations and example, in order to gain acceptance.

Finally, do not let your child live with you like a guest or visitor – unable to freely express themselves for fear of offending or upsetting you. Enable your child to express himself or herself before you without fear of intimidation, ridicule or rejection.

## 3. What are the best methods of training up a child?

It is very important that children are trained in the right way, otherwise it will be a waste of time. The child will soon forget the training if it isn't done correctly.

Two good methods of bringing up children are:

**A - By example.** Obviously, this means that your own life must demonstrate to your children what you expect them to practise as they grow up. If you don't want your children to behave in a certain way, then, don't let them see that behaviour in you. You should demonstrate at home the good attributes you want your children to develop.

In Genesis 18:19, God says that He has chosen Abraham so that he will instruct his descendants by doing what is right and just himself. That is, Abraham will lead by example.

Abraham demonstrated to his household what he wanted them to become as they grew up. Abraham used his lifestyle to practically teach his children how to live a life of faith in the Lord. His son Isaac saw it in him, and as a result lived a life of faith when he grew up.

It would be great if every parent had this kind of testimony about their example. As a parent, you must realise that whatever your child sees in you he or she is very likely to practise it, and even do it better than you, when that child grows up.

For example, if your son or daughter catches you lying, he or she is likely to grow up to lie even better than you. Therefore, it is important that you let your children see in you whatever you expect them to become in the future. If you want your children to grow up to love God, or love Him even more than you, then, show them that you love God. Words aren't enough. It needs practical demonstration.

In the Bible, Timothy grew up to practise the same faith that he saw in his grandmother and mother, as testified by Paul: *When I call to remembrance the unfeigned faith that is in thee, which dwelt first in thy grandmother Lois, and thy mother Eunice; and I am persuaded that in thee also"* (2 Timothy 1:5).

The best method to pass instruction to someone else is by example. People do not usually forget what they practically encountered.

**B - Counselling.** This involves sitting down with your children and talking to them, to explain the best thing to do in certain circumstances.

For example, Proverbs 2:1 teaches children to receive the words of their parents and treasure their commands, so that they can *"find the knowledge of God"* (verse 5). This is encouraging children to follow the advice of their parents.

One of the advantages of sitting down with a child to give him or her counsel is that it causes change to happen from the inside. 'Barking orders' at a child may get temporary results from fear, but it won't create positive inner change. Regular counselling done with love will plant good moral values inside the child.

This is important, because for any child to change for the better, that change has to first start from inside. Until the training penetrates the heart, you can't expect positive changes on the outside.

As a parent, you must spend quality time with your child, regularly giving biblical teaching and counselling. Through such regular communication, the changes begin to develop from inside the child until they manifest outside the child through his or her character and behaviour.

## 4. Possible factors that could hinder training

For effective home training, we must identify and eliminate factors that may hinder it. These include:

A - **Anger.** Training up a child under the influence of anger manifests in hostility and displeasure towards the child. Under such a situation, instructions and correction are done with a wrong spirit. It communicates hatred instead of love. It frightens the child and gives a wrong impression. Parenting will be seen as a fight instead of a help to build up a child's character.

It is imperative for parents to understand that an instruction clouded by the spirit of anger does not cause positive, permanent change. Instead, it causes deception. This is because when a child comes under the attack of an angry parent, the child will design a method of escape by pretending to be good. The child will start pretending to be what he or she is not, in order to avoid being told off or punished again. This makes the child better at deception and defeats the whole point of the training.

The child will also grow up with emotional damage. A child that is emotionally damaged will develop a wrong interpretation of life, due to the negative environment he or she was raised in. That is why Colossians 3:21 advises parents not to provoke their children to anger, as this will only discourage them.

And anger begets anger. When you bring up a child under the influence of anger it's no surprise if the child also becomes angry.

Such a child may obey their parents for a while, but with anger. And then when they are older, that anger will come out in wrong ways.

James 1:20 says that *"the wrath of man worketh not the righteousness of God"*. This implies that nothing good can be achieved under anger. Anger will only help you to mess up a situation that could have produced a godly outcome if it had been conducted with a right attitude.

B - **Corrupt words.** Ephesians 4:29 admonishes us to avoid speaking corrupt words to each other: Let no corrupt communication proceed out of your mouth, but that which is good to the use of edifying, that it may minister grace unto the hearers.

This is also applicable to parenting. Corrupt communication includes abusive words, calling children bad names, cursing them, swearing at them, using insulting words, demeaning words, threatening words, etc. Corrupt words damage a child emotionally and create a perverted picture of who the child is inside the child. The child begins to see her or himself in the light of the words spoken by the parents.

Some children grow up hating themselves because of wrong words planted in their spirits by their parents while growing up. Some children have no self-confidence because of the terrible words they received from their parents.

Unfortunately, if the situation persists long enough, it may influence the child to become an abusive parent later in life.

C - **Intimidation.** This is parenting by threat, using the weapon of fear. It is designed to coerce a child into submission. Parents that use intimidation as a method of parenting usually frighten the child with the negative consequences of disobeying their instructions. The child obeys not because he or she loves the parent but because of fear of the consequences of disobedience.

Now, there is a place for fear of punishment as an aid for discipline. But it must be made clear to the child that punishment comes from a heart of regret not enjoyment, that the parent does not want to punish but has to in order to be loving. Children must see that punishment is given out of love and a desire to help children improve themselves, not out of vindictiveness or hatred. And intimidation must not be involved – you must explain rationally and calmly that there are consequences to disobedience, but not be threatening and angry.

If parenting is motivated by love, then using intimidation to parent a child raises a concern. This is because, according to 1 JOHN 4:18, fear and love don't go together: *There is no fear in love; but perfect love casteth out fear: because fear hath torment. He that feareth is not made perfect in love.*

Careful discipline is necessary, as it says in PROVERBS 13:24: *He that spareth his rod hateth his son: but he that loveth him chasteneth him betimes. But intimidation will do more damage than good to a child.*

For example, a child trained under intimidation will develop low self-esteem. Such a child will lack the boldness needed to succeed in life. When you intimidate a child, you kill him from inside. A child's potential and self-confidence can be destroyed by intimidation.

Unfortunately, a child that grows up under intimidation can appear obedient and gentle to the parents, but when freed from parental control, can go completely off the rails. Alternatively, the parents are unknowingly developing such low self-esteem and courage that when the child grows up, he or she will not be able to deal with the pressures of the world.

D - **Zombie-inducing parenting style.** 'Zombies' are fictional characters that are dead people with no souls – no ability to think for themselves, but just operate on instinct. When we talk about real people as zombies, we mean people who are just driven along by the crowd and have no individuality or independence. They appear to lack the capacity to take decisions or make choices for themselves.

Some parents treat their children as if they are zombies or unintelligent creatures. They don't expect their children to make choices or decisions, so they do it all for them. Of course, when children are babies they need to have everything done for them, but as children grow up they need to be allowed to do more for themselves. Instead, zombifying parents continue to dictate everything for their children.

Such children grow up in like dummies or zombies, not able to act without asking parents what they should do, or expecting parents to continue doing lots for them even when they are adults themselves.

Good parenting involves the child in the parenting. Allow your children to make certain decisions – initially under your supervision, but then later without your involvement. Let them take risks, so long as you can ensure the consequences are not serious even if they make the wrong decisions.

Do not dictate everything to your child, otherwise you will hinder his mental capacity from developing and you will not be preparing the child for independent life. Your child is not an inanimate object but a complete creature of God, with all the necessary capacity to live an independent life.

(Unless they suffer from a severe disability of some kind, of course.) Do not be a dictator in parenting. Engage the child in their own development.

E - **Neglect.** The prophet Eli was accused of neglect in parenting his two sons. The situation was so serious that God had to judge Eli for it:

*For I have told him that I will judge his house for ever for the iniquity which he knoweth; because his sons made themselves vile, and he restrained them not.* 1 SAMUEL 3:13.

God tells Samuel that Eli has committed neglect by constantly ignoring the errors of his two sons.

Some parents do not pay enough attention to their children's character development. Such parents fail in their moral obligation towards their children. Unfortunately, parents that neglect their children's character usually give reasons to justify their inaction. Such reasoning may include the excuse that the child is stubborn and so it is a waste of time to parent such a child.

Alternatively, some parents have delegated their responsibility to the State. They hope that the law of the land or the society's norms will teach their children lessons that they refused to accept from their parents. This is a big mistake. It is impossible to make a bad situation better by doing nothing.

Parents of stubborn children should search their conscience to see where they have got it wrong in parenting. It is possible that the parents have done something wrong that led to the child's stubbornness, or they failed to intervene at an early stage when stubbornness was developing. Undoubtedly, some children are more stubborn than others, but that doesn't mean you give up – it just means you have to work harder or get wiser as a parent by seeking help and advice from others.

F - **The qualification of a trainer.** A woman brought her child to a friend to help her counsel the child to stop eating chocolate. The friend told the woman to come back in a few days' time. She consented, and after a few days returned to her friend's house. Her friend then gave counselling to the child to stop eating chocolate.

When the woman was about to leave her friend's house, she asked her friend why she did not say the same thing to the child the last time they came. Her friend told her that the first time the mother came round with her child, she was still eating chocolate herself and felt morally unqualified to advise someone else to stop something she was doing herself.

MATHEW 7:3-4 states that you are not qualified to remove the speck from your brother's eye when you have a plank in your own eye.

You are not ready to train a child to drop a certain bad habit if you are not able to control that habit yourself. For example, a father that lies is not morally qualified to train a child not to lie. You have to stop telling lies first before you can train your child to stop telling lies. Of course, you can tell them to stop, but if they find out that you lie, you will have completely undermined your teaching – as well as their respect for you.

Similarly, you can't tell your children to stop arguing with each other if they see you and your spouse always arguing with each other. You must understand that for parenting to work, there is a moral condition to fulfil. Your children will not take you seriously if you fail to practise what you preach.

## 5. Topics for training

As a Christian parent, the golden rule for training up children is this: instruct them in God's word and ensure that your demands and expectations are biblical.

Let your children see that whatever you demand from them doesn't come from you but from the word of God. You don't want to give them the impression that you are a selfish dictator, commanding them to satisfy your own wants or needs. Let them know that you didn't make the rules. Point your children towards God always, not yourself.

This is important because your children will not always have you by their side, but God will always be with them if they serve Him. It is only God who can be with your children 24/7, not yourself. It is wise to always point your children to seek God's way for the right way to live.

So, what are the most important things to teach your child?

While it is important to teach the whole counsel of God as revealed in His word, there are some overarching themes that need specific emphasis as you bring up your children in the way they should go.

Examples are:

- A - **The love of God.** Let your children know that God loves them. Constantly create the picture of God's love towards them in their hearts from the outset. This will inspire them to love God in return. 1 JOHN 4:19 says: *We love him, because he first loved us.*

- B - **The benefits of serving God.** Encourage your children to get involved in the church activities and let them see you serving God. Let your children know the benefits of serving God. Share many testimonies of your life with them to motivate them in serving Him.

- C - **The fear of God.** Let them know that to fear God is wise, because He is a God of love but He is also holy and will punish evil. Let them know that God will judge sinners and evildoers in the next life. You can use PROVERBS 1:7 to teach them more about this.

D - **The benefits of faith.** Teach them about the miracle-working power of God. Psalm 78:4 states that we should tell the next generation about the wonderful works of God. This will build up their trust in God. Tell them about the miracles and answers to prayer that you have experienced or know have happened. Sow seeds of faith inside your children consistently as they grow up.

E - **The benefits of obedience.** Let them know the blessings of doing the right things in life. This will make obedience attractive to your children. Let them also know the dangers of doing the wrong things. See Proverbs 14:12.

F - **The joy of servanthood.** Let them know that it is more beneficial to serve than to be served. Let them serve others at home. Similarly, let your children see you serving at home, at church and in your community. Let them see you doing house work, kitchen work, garden work, fixing things at home, etc. Let them see you helping their mother or father.

Help your children in many situations to see that you really enjoy serving your fellow human beings. Most of the rebellious nature we see in children these days started from home in a subtle manner.

G - **The reality of conflict.** Let them know that it is inevitable that they will not be able to please everybody all of the time! People will argue with them, oppose them and offend them, and they must learn to forgive. And just as other people will offend them, they will also offend others – even if by accident.

Let your children know the truth that their relationships with fellow human beings can never be perfect because there are inherent weaknesses in human beings, which bring friction in their interactions. Raise your children to forgive and not to bear grudges, harbour bitterness or seek revenge. Let this practice start from home when your child has an issue with siblings or friends. Encourage forgiveness and reconciliation, and never blindly support your child against the person who has wronged him or her.

**H - The spiritual law of cause and effect.** Let them know that whatever a man sows he will reap. Plant in the hearts of your children the determination never to do evil, if they do not want evil to come to them.

**I - Teach your children the golden rule of life.** The golden rule (LUKE 6:31) requires that you do to others what you want them to do to you. That is, if you want people to treat you well, then, you also must treat them well. Teach your children that whatever they expect from people, they must first give to people. They should give love if they want to be loved. They must be a friend in order to make friends.

**J - Teach your children the benefits of good education.** Do not just ensure that your children get a good education but let them know the benefits of it for the world in which they live. Explain the importance of education to them, that it will help them find a good job and understand the world around them, and make them more useful to family, society, government and the God who created them.

**K - Teach your children to obey authority.** Teach them to obey you, but explain the benefits of being obedient. If they learn to obey authority in the home, they will be more likely to obey the authorities and laws of the country as an adult. Let your children see you obey the law of the land – including common traffic regulations like the speed limit.

**L - Teach your children what life has taught you.** Share your story with your children. Let your children learn from you. PROVERBS 5:1 says: My son, attend unto my wisdom, and bow thine ear to my understanding. Let them learn from your mistakes so that they will not make the same errors. Let them also learn from your success, so that they can make good decisions in the future. Teach your children the practical things life has taught you.

M - **Teach your children to honour their parents.** Exodus 20:12 says: *Honour thy father and thy mother: that thy days may be long upon the land which the LORD thy God giveth thee.*

A child who dishonours his or her parents will dishonour whoever comes into his or her life. Teach your children the importance of honour and respect, especially for parents. Let them know that honour begets honour – if you show respect to others, you will receive respect. Intentionally bring up your children to be respectful and humble in life.

N - **Teach your children to make the word of God their standard.** Pass the word of God to your children as an eternal heritage. Educate and show them how to make the word of God a standard for living. Teach them that the word of God is the only book that can never be obsolete or become irrelevant. Teach them how to apply the word of God to their situations.

## Four

# COMMON MISTAKES PARENTS MAKE ABOUT THEIR CHILDREN

*Even so it is not the will of your Father which is in heaven, that one of these little ones should perish.*
MATTHEW 18:14.

God values children. He does not want them to be lost. Unfortunately, many parents lead their children astray by the way they bring them up.

In this chapter we will examine some of the common errors some parents make that damage their children's upbringing.

## 1. They allow their children to be brought up by other people

For different reasons (sometimes caused by the pressures of life), some parents ask another couple or individual to look after their children, and the children go and live with them for a time. In some situations, this becomes a permanent arrangement, or the children are moved on again and again to other family members when situations change.

This is never the ideal way to raise your children, and can be a really bad error. The more that a child is moved around from one carer to the next, the more their 'guidance' keeps changing, and the more likely it is that they will grow up with emotional problems or confusion. This is because such a child will be exposed to different teaching and beliefs about life. Also, such a child is vulnerable to exploitation. Some people treat children that are not theirs differently from their own children, sometimes cruelly so.

While it is true that some parents can be abusive towards their own children, the chance of this occurrence is low compared with children living with other parents.

Raise your children yourself, if at all possible. Don't give your parenting responsibilities to other parents unless you become physically incapable of parenting due to a severe illness. There is nobody that can substitute for you in the lives of your children.

## 2. They transfer to their children a wrong spirit that dwells in them

For example, some parents suffer from malice or bitterness. Unfortunately, they transfer these bad spirits into the lives of their children unknowingly. Such parents encourage their children to seek revenge or stop playing with friends who have wronged them. Indirectly, they are teaching their children to be controlled by the offences of life, instead of controlling their response to offences.

Instead of teaching and showing their children the power of love and forgiveness, they show them the path of hatred and hostility. The wrong spirits that have limited the parents start to limit their children.

Similarly, some parents suffer from a lying spirit. Such parents may teach their children lies as a way of escape from certain problems. In so doing, they indirectly invite the lying spirit that dwells in them into the lives of their children. Such children grow up in life suffering from the same faults that troubled their parents' lives.

## 3. They ignore warning signals concerning their children

Some parents don't take seriously the symptoms of abnormal behaviour in their children. Usually, before a character fault becomes a serious problem in the life of a child, there are some warning signals. These signs in a child's behaviour are a message to the parents that the problem needs their urgent attention. But some parents don't get it until it is too late. Never ignore warning signals about your children that manifest in their behaviour. Act before it becomes too late.

## 4. They compare their children with other parents' children

Every child is unique. There are no two children that will be exactly the same. When you compare your children with other children, you will lose focus on God's plans for your children. You may end up raising your children using another parent's style as a parenting model, which may not be appropriate for your own children. Also, a child that is constantly being told that he or she is not as good as his or her peers will not be happy. Such a child may grow up with low self-esteem or resentment of other children.

## 5. They choose a career for their children

Some parents choose what their children will do in life before they are even old enough to show talent in that area. They don't let their children choose what they want to be in life; they choose for them. Such children end up doing what God did not create them for. They do what they have no interest or joy in. They enter into a career just to please their parents. It is an error.

Never choose a career for your child. You can give guidance and share your experience, but never impose a career path on a child.

## 6. They practise parenting by intimidation

Parenting should be done with love. But some parents don't know how to train up a child with love, and instead use the weapons of fear, threat and intimidation. Some parents even use harassment and bullying as a means of parenting.

The children of such parents obey them not because they want to, but because of fear of their parents. They pretend to be obedient. When such children are left alone, they return to their normal character. They only obey their parents to please them, not because they have any conviction about doing wrong or the rightness of obedience.

Only genuine love can change a person for the better, not hatred or fear. Parenting by love involves no threat, intimidation or harassment. Of course there needs to be discipline and appropriate punishments that are fair and proportionate, but administered in a spirit of love not an atmosphere of intimidation.

## 7. They build walls between themselves and their children

Some parents give no freedom to their children to enjoy their company. They only communicate with their children when they have to tell them to do something, or to stop them doing something. Such children aren't allowed the privilege of asking their parents questions to find out things. Their parents give instruction through dictation and show no interest in their children's views. They don't let their children voice their own opinions about things that concern their lives. Unfortunately, such children search for answers to their questions in the wrong places. As a parent, create a forum through which your children can relate with you as friends, not as slaves.

## 8. They don't give their children emotional support

Children who have been bullied by friends or treated badly by outsiders need support from their parents. Children need empathy. They need parents that will encourage them when they are discouraged. Children need to be strengthened and have their spirits lifted up, especially when they fail in certain things, such as their education.

Some parents only criticise their children when they go wrong; they don't know how to move on from that and encourage their children so that they can do better next time. Such children will end up hiding their failures and faults from their parents so as to escape their criticism.

## 9. They expose their children to things at the wrong age

There are some facts or situations that your children will not be able to handle because they have not been prepared for such things. Before you give some information or expose your children to certain experiences, be sure that they can cope with it. What a child of ten years can handle should not be shared with a child of five.

For example, children should not be left in front of the TV without you knowing what is on will be appropriate for their age group. But there are also situations in real life that a child should not be exposed to, according to the level of maturity, and emotional and psychological development. Do not take your children to events they are not yet mature enough to witness.

## 10. They don't know who their children associate with

You must not be too busy not to know who your children are spending time with. You must know as much as possible about your children's friends. Wrong associations can corrupt good character. The older they get, the more your children will be influenced by their friends and acquaintances. They will have a great influence on their character, so try to encourage good choices about friendships.

## 11. They love their children differently

It is wrong for a parent to treat children differently. Even if you have a special interest in one of your children, or find it easier to get on with one of them than the others, you must not let the others know. If children get the impression that their parents love them less than another sibling, it will cause envy and hatred. This will lead to enmity among your children.

## 12. They don't know the temperament of their children

Someone's temperament is the manner of thinking, behaving, or reacting that is characteristic of that person. This is particularly to do with the way our moods affect our behaviour. If you know someone's temperament, you can take a reasonable guess at how they will behave under certain circumstances, or if you know their moods you will know how they are likely to react when when in one mood or the other.

Parents must know the temperament of their children, but not just so that you can anticipate how they will react to situations. Knowing your child will also enable you to know how to help him or her undergo character adjustment while still young. For example, if you notice that violent anger or a vengeful tendency occurs when a child is upset, worried or depressed, then you need to look at what is causing that upset and how to avoid it or deal with it. If you just condemn the symptom without addressing the cause, then you won't solve the problem.

Some of the character problems in many adults could be due to a lack of parental assistance while they were young.

## 13. They don't know the pains of their children

If you don't know what is paining your children you are not likely to be able to offer them help. You should know what makes them sad or angry, and what demotivates them. You should know what makes your children cry or get stressed. Your children may be suffering in silence without telling you, because they think that you are not interested in their world.

## 14. They show no interest in making their children happy

Some parents are so wrapped up in their own issues that they don't take an interest in what makes their children happy. So long as their children behave, that's all that matters to them. But children want their parents to do things that will make them happy. Your children will be happy when you buy them what they like and take them out for play and fun experiences.

That doesn't mean they should get everything they want without any effort on their part, or you will spoil them, but it does mean looking to their needs more your own. That is the sacrifice parents must make if they are to be successful parents. Children who grow up with happiness will transfer it to whoever they come across in life. Such children become adults who everybody wants to befriend.

## 15. They are bad examples to their children

Some parents fight each other in the presence of their children, indirectly teaching them that marriage is about fighting and that it is not something they want for themselves in the future. Some parents even allow their children to see their bad habits, such as smoking, swearing or drinking too much alcohol. Some parents have no credibility in the eyes of their children because they have become a bad influence on them. A parent that tells lies has no credibility when instructing his child not to lie.

## 16. They speak carelessly to their children

Some parents curse their children or continually use abusive words about them. Parents have a certain spiritual authority over their children, so if curses are spoken into the life of a child, they have the potential to come true. Soon, the child will develop according to the word of his or her parent. For example, if you keep calling your child lazy; they will grow up thinking that they are lazy and that there is nothing they can do about it – that's just how they are. Instead, tell your child that; "that was a lazy thing to do" rather than saying "you are lazy".

Stop speaking wrong words to your children. In Genesis 49, every word Jacob spoke into the lives of his children came to pass.

## 17. They are violent towards their children

Some parents are very aggressive towards their children. Some parents even beat their children. A child brought up under a violent atmosphere will grow up with emotional problems, and learn to be violent towards others. Aggressive parents are likely to produce aggressive children. Due to their vulnerability, children should be brought up under calmness. Parents should demonstrate to their children that tempers can be controlled, and that there are better ways of dealing with problems than violence.

## 18. They fail to build bonds with their children

Some parents do not connect with their children nor build friendly relationships with them. Such children grow up without any emotional connection to their parents and find that frustrating, because deep down inside they feel deprived of the relationship that they should have. Not only that, but also children from such families find it difficult to build friendships with others, and to relate to their own children.

## 19. They don't recognise that their children are emulating them

Directly or indirectly, you are influencing your children's character development. Your children will grow up to show some of your moral weaknesses as well as your strengths. Beware of the way you live before your children, because you are influencing them for good or ill.

## 20. They think they can change their children's character by force

It is only love that can positively influence a fellow human being. You can't change your child's character by force. This is because what makes your child act as he or she does comes from inside, not outside of the child. Love can touch what no human hand can touch.

## 21. They are too busy to spend quality time with them

Parenting needs time. Many parents have no time for their children. They claim to be too busy, and often compensate by buying things for their children – when in fact their children need their attention not the latest phone or toy. But the reality is that the parents have no time for their children's upbringing because they have not made it a priority. They have put work or their leisure interests, or even their church work, before their children. That is always wrong. Do not produce children you will not have time – or will not make time – to raise.

## 22. They show them no respect

You must have respect for your children. You must respect their individuality and their uniqueness, rather than expecting them to be like any other child. Whatever you respect, you will treat gently and with caution. Your children are human beings. They have emotions. They want honour. They want to feel important and relevant in your life. They want to see that you value their presence around you.

Help your children to develop a sense of self-value as they grow up. Help them to develop a good self-esteem. Do not dehumanise your children. Never treat your children as less important than something else.

## 23. They support their child against the outsider even when the child is in the wrong

Taking your child's side even when they have done wrong is the wrong way to show that you love your children. Let your children know that they were wrong when they were wrong, yet you love them all the same. Let your children see that you can't compromise the truth. Let them know that you will always be frank with them in all situations, and then they will trust you.

## 24. They give them too much freedom too young

A child needs a lot of control when young, for his or her own safety and because they have a lot to learn. But the older they get, the more freedom they should be given to explore things for themselves, take risks and make mistakes. This is the only way that they will learn some things for themselves, understand the meaning of personal responsibility and understand that their actions have consequences.

But don't make the mistake of giving them too much freedom too early. For example, to let a ten-year-old decide whether or not to drink alcohol is not appropriate. This is because such a child has not grown to the age where he or she can make informed decisions; they will not understand the consequences of the decision.

## 25. They sometimes over-discipline their children

There is the opposite of too much freedom – too little freedom. Don't stifle you children so that they fail to develop their own self-discipline. And if you discipline your child for too many trivial things, they will think they are permanently under your anger and disapproval, and that you care more about something like a broken glass than you do about them.

And make sure your level of discipline is commensurate with the offence. If the punishment is too big and outweighs the offence committed, it creates a wrong impression in the mind of children. They think you are being vindictive and cruel. As a parent, be reasonable in correction.

## 26. They leave them unsupervised

Apart from the obvious physical dangers that may threaten a child's safety if there is a lack of supervision, there are also psychological consequences.

It is a mistake to allow children to be unsupervised in order to make mistakes so that they will learn from them, when they are at the wrong age to be able to handle such adult thinking. To expose them to situations that could damage them psychologically could be described as an act of wickedness. It is certainly callous if you purposely leave your children alone to struggle with what you know is beyond their ability. The consequences may be far worse than you expect.

Do not set your child up for failure as that may make them feel that they are a failure, which can lead to self-loathing, and even self-harm and depression in later life. Don't watch your child fail if there is something you can do to help.

## 27. They focus only on the weaknesses of their children

You do not want your child to grow up only being aware of his or her weaknesses. Children need to know they have strengths too. Do not just talk to your children about the problems they have, but praise them for their abilities and achievements. Let your child know what he or she is capable of doing, as well as what he or she is not capable of doing. But even then, remind your child that we can change, and that some of our weaknesses – especially the sinful ones – can be overcome.

## 28. They don't take their promises to their children seriously

Some parents do not realise that words matter. Such parents make promises to their children but often fail to fulfil them. As a result, their children see a lack of integrity in them and lose trust in them. If you lose integrity before your children, it will be difficult for them to take you seriously in life. Do not promise what you can't fulfil, but make every effort to keep your promises.

## 29. They transfer anger

Some parents who have spouses who hurt them, whether emotionally or physically, tend to take it out on their children. This can be manifested in a variety of ways, from physical abuse to minor verbal assaults. This is a transfer of anger. The children suffer for the sins of their parents. This can reproduce hatred in your offspring that will be transferred from generation to generation, if not halted. Never punish your children as a way of letting out your anger against your spouse.

Sometimes this happens at a sub-conscious level, so you need to be extra vigilant about your emotions and motives. Remember that your children are innocent of whatever might have taken place between you and their mother or father, and it is unfair to allow your own frustrations to overflow onto your children.

## 30. They delay proper parenting

*Chasten thy son while there is hope, and let not thy soul spare for his crying.* PROVERBS 19:18.

The time of hope for chastening a child is when the child is still young. When the child has reached adulthood, it is too late to start parenting. What you fail to teach your child at a lower age is unlikely to be teachable at an older age. Good parenting becomes almost impossible when it hasn't been in place from an early age.

## 31. They delay dealing with rivalry between their children

Some children grow up hating each other because their parents failed to address this abnormality while they were young. As a parent, whenever you notice any sign of conflict between your children, you must deal with it without delay. Promote love between your children while they are still under your control, so that when they grow up, they will keep on loving each other.

## 32. They named their children after negative incidences or experiences

Some parents name their children to express certain events that have taken place in their lives. They want to keep the memory alive, but they indirectly attach the destiny of their children to the negative occurrence in their lives. Therefore, the spirit that sponsored the bad event may gain entrance into the lives of such children to manipulate their destinies.

Similarly, some parents name their children after a dead relative. Unfortunately, this may be a family tradition but it can establish a demonic 'soul-tie' between the innocent child and the dead relative, if that relative allowed some kind of evil into their life. Therefore, as a parent, before you give names to your children, seek the counsel of the God who gives the children to you.

## 33. They fail to study their children to find out their interests, gifts, uniqueness and future potential.

As a parent it is your responsibility to help your child discover his or her uniqueness, so that you can give proper advice to the child – especially when it comes to formal education. Knowing your child's potential and capabilities will enable you to know how to guide the child in his or her education. For example, if you know the strengths and weaknesses of your children, you will also know at an early stage the kind of help they will need to find their place in life. Study your child.

## 34. They develop wrong expectations regarding their children

Some parents just believe that their children will do well despite not investing anything good into the lives of their children. This is fantasy. If you expect the future of your children to be bright, you have to put time and effort into their lives.

## 35. They withhold their children from God

Some parents think that church activities are only for adults, and leave their children at home while they attend services. Some parents even prevent their children from being used by God, because they don't take their children seriously when they express a desire to serve God in some way.

Yet, God can speak through the mouths of children (PSALM 8:2) and Jesus told us not to prevent children from coming to him (Matthew 19:14). You must always appear before God with your children. Encourage your children to worship, love and serve God.

# Five

## PARENTING BY LOVE

*He that loveth not knoweth not God; for God is love.*
1 John 4:8.

God is love. Godly love is 'agape' – an unconditional love. It is the love that makes God relate with humanity in the way that He does.

In Matthew 6:9, Jesus taught us to pray to God as a father: *After this manner therefore pray ye: Our Father which art in heaven, hallowed be thy name...* So if God is a parent and God is love, then it follows that God parents with love.

Since the time of creation, God has been relating with mankind in the role of a parent. Therefore, to understand the expectations of God regarding our own parenting, we need to explore how God relates to his children – us! This will give us a better understanding of how we should parent our children. This will be our standard as regards parenting.

In this chapter we will look at some of the basic attributes of parenting with love, using God as a standard.

## 1. Love makes itself known

At the beginning of His relationship with Moses, God made Himself known to him. In EXODUS 3:6, God revealed who He is. In EXODUS 20, God revealed His likes and dislikes. God did not assume that the Israelites would know His rules and regulations. He taught them.

As a parent, you must make yourself known to your children. Let them know your tastes and your standards – what you approve and disapprove of. Do not assume that your children will know your expectations by instinct. Do not let your children wander around trying to figure out what you like or dislike. Love makes itself known to save others from unknowingly falling into error. This is love.

## 2. Love reveals its purpose

In GENESIS 12:1-3 God revealed to Abraham His purpose for his life. This was to motivate Abraham and to convince him that his life was in good hands. God did not assume that Abraham knew that He is a good God and that He would take good care of his life. God revealed to Abraham what He had in mind for his life.

As a parent, motivate your children by revealing to them your purpose for them. Let them know that you mean well for their lives. Tell them what you hope their future is like. Naturally, a person is likely to behave well toward somebody he knows to have his best interests at heart. Create a good picture of tomorrow in the mind of your children. This will settle their anxiety about your intention towards them, especially when you discipline them. This is love.

## 3. Love meets needs

NEHEMIAH 9:20-21 reveals that God provided food, water, shelter, clothing and other needs for Israel for 40 years. This is love. Love provides all needs, not just some, whether they are social, emotional, material, financial, etc.

As a parent, you must attend to all the needs of your children. Your children do not just need food and a bed but all the other basic things for a decent life. Pray that God will bless you so that you will be able to meet all the needs of your children. A child who lacks the basic needs of life will be tempted to look to other people for those needs – leaving them vulnerable to adults or peers who make promises in order to exploit them.

## 4. Love explains the secrets of success

In Joshua 1:8, God told Joshua what he had to do in order to succeed in life. This is love. God wished him well in life. God wants us to succeed in life too.

As a parent, it is your responsibility to educate your children about life and all you've learned about how to succeed. It is also your role to help your children to solve problems that come their way. You must be an adviser and a counsellor to your children. Share wisdom with them. Let your children grow up knowing that you are doing all you can to help them in life.

## 5. Love motivates

In Zechariah 4:7, God sent a word of encouragement and motivation to Zerubbabel, saying that he would overcome the obstacles before him. Love motivates. Love speaks words of encouragement. When days are dark, love gives assurance that there is light at the end of every tunnel. As a parent, your role includes giving motivation and encouragement to your children, especially when they face challenges. Avoid actions that demotivate your children.

## 6. Love addresses evil

In 1 Kings 21:17-24, God sent the prophet Elijah to King Ahab to condemn the evil that Ahab had done to Naboth. In 2 Samuel 12:7-14, God did the same thing – sending the prophet Nathan to King David when he committed adultery and murder. Love never keeps quiet or remains silent about evil. Love will speak out when evil is committed. As a parent, never ignore evil committed by your children. You must address every sin your children commit as quickly as possible. This will save the soul of your children from destruction. Never indulge your children in their wrong habits.

## 7. Love uses 'the rod of men' to punish

2 SAMUEL 7:14-15 says: *I will be his father, and he shall be my son. If he commit iniquity, I will chasten him with the rod of men, and with the stripes of the children of men: but my mercy shall not depart away from him, as I took it from Saul...*

God promised David that if He needed to discipline his son, He would use men to bring punishment to him, but he would not withdraw his mercy, like he did from King Saul. Saul was killed in battle because of his disobedience, and the monarchy was taken from his family. But God promised David that his son, Solomon, would receive a lesser punishment and not be killed, and that the line of kings would continue with Solomon's descendants.

So, God's punishment of Solomon would be gentle and restricted. God's discipline of his children today is always for their good – he does not destroy them (HEBREWS 12:10). So, when we discipline our children, it must be gentle and intended for their good. It must not be destructive, but constructive. That is 'the rod of men'. In punishment, love must still be the motivation and the controlling factor.

As a parent, whenever you have to correct your children for wrongdoing, use 'the rod of men'. The intention of correction is to make the child better, not to destroy the child. That is love.

## 8. Love shows understanding

PSALM 103:14 states that God remembers that men are made from dust – in other words, that we are not perfect. Imperfection will remain as long as this world still exists. Love shows understanding. Love knows what it is dealing with.

As a parent you must not demand perfection of your children – you must recognise that they are human and will have weaknesses. In addition, they are not adults, so don't treat them like adults. Do not set a standard that only an adult could satisfy. That would be unfair and unloving.

## 9. Love is forgiving

PSALM 103:9 tells us that God does not stay angry for ever. When any of His children annoy Him and He gets angry, it will be for a short time. That is love. As a parent, let your anger towards your children be short-lived. Show your children that you are forgiving, so that they can imitate you. Once your child's disobedience has been dealt with through a moderate punishment, drop the issue – don't keep complaining to the child about it. Do not keep reminding your children of things they did wrong days ago. If you continue, you will embitter him or her towards you. Forgiving is love.

## 10. Love is merciful

PSALM 103:13 states that God pities His children. Pity makes Him intervene when one of His children is heading towards danger. Pity makes Him show compassion towards His children. Pity makes Him not punish His children as their sins deserve. The vulnerability of a child should draw compassion from the parent. So as a parent, show pity towards your children. Be considerate. Always give them another chance, even when they blow the first one and the second one. Always be ready to help your children, even when they fail to ask for it. That is love.

## 11. Love promotes reconciliation

In JOB 42:7-11, God organised a reconciliation between Job and his friends. As a parent, you must ensure peace among your children. You must never allow enmity to grow among them. You must be an agent of peace between your children. When your children offend each other, you must intervene to bring them back together. You must never support one child against the other. You must maintain a balanced relationship between all your children. Love is an agent of peace.

## 12. Love appreciates love

In 1 KINGS 3:3-5, God showed His appreciation for the act of love King Solomon showed by sacrificing a thousand animals to the Lord. God recognised Solomon's love for Him.

As a parent, you must always appreciate every act of love your children show towards you, and show appreciate for their obedience. You must be quick to say thank you to your children whenever they do something good. Tell your children "Well done!" whenever they make an effort to do something good. Let your children see gratefulness in you, for them to imitate.

## 13. Love announces good news

In LUKE 1:19, God sent good news to His people to give them hope for the future. Good news makes people happy. God wants to make His people happy and give them reasons to rejoice.

As a parent, intentionally choose to make your children happy. Tell them the good news of something exciting or fun that you are planning for them. Share good stories with them to make them happy. Good news will make your children be naturally drawn to you. Good news is medicinal; it strengthens the bones. Love is good and always brings something good.

## 14. Love answers questions

In ACTS 9:6, God answered a question that Paul asked. He did not ignore Paul but gave him a clear answer. Love will never leave a person in the dark.

As a parent, be ready to supply answers to your children's questions. Not only that, but create an atmosphere that will encourage your children to ask you questions. Be friendly to your children. Let them know the reasons for your demands and instructions. Ask your children questions and enable them to ask you in return. That is love.

## 15. Love is evidence-based

Love does not make up an explanation. Love acts on evidence, not assumptions. In GENESIS 22:1-16, God put Abraham through a test that would prove Abraham's love for Him. God didn't rely on hearsay or conjecture. Whatever God says about any of His children is based on solid evidence.

As a parent, be evidenced-based in dealing with your children. A lack of evidence creates doubt. Never put your children in a position of doubt. Never accuse your children of something without credible evidence to back it up. Don't just assume they have done something wrong because they have done it before. Give them the benefit of the doubt. Never tell your children what you are not sure of yourself.

## 16. Love promotes liberty

Where there is love, there is freedom. Love allows people to be free to speak, act, plan and make their own choices. Love allows people to be real and genuine. In DEUTERONOMY 30:19, God gave Israel the freedom to make choices. This allowed them to be real and show their true colours as a people.

As a parent, you must let your children enjoy liberty (to the degree that is appropriate for their age). Allow your children to be real and to show their true character. This will help you to know them well enough to be able to help them improve. Where there is no liberty, people will pretend to be who they are not. Though it is necessary to limit your children's freedoms, they must not be turned into robots that function only under programmed guidance.

## 17. Love gives warnings

When love foresees danger it warns those who might fall into it. In MATTHEW 2:13, God told Jesus' parents to flee to Egypt because Herod wanted to kill Jesus. God's word warns us of the evils and traps that we can fall into.

As a parent, you must be clear with your children about the dangers they face. You don't need to go into all the details if they are young, but they must be told. Children are naïve and most are easily tricked or led astray. And even older children need to be warned about the predicaments they face. Whether they reject your advice or not – it is your responsibility to warn them. Love does not allow children to be hurt or endangered just in order to teach them a lesson. Genuine love explains the hidden dangers so that children will be alert to them. Never withhold beneficial information from your children.

## 18. Love is sacrificial

Love is always ready to do whatever it takes to express itself. In JOHN 3:16, God offered Jesus, His only begotten Son, to live as a man and die for the people He loves. As a parent, do whatever you can to help your children grow up to be Christlike. Be ready to pay any price necessary for your children to have a better future. That is love.

## Six

# COUNSEL FROM THE SCRIPTURES

The word of God reveals all the principles necessary for parenting. This chapter brings you some extracts from the revelational knowledge of the scriptures to assist you in raising your children according to God's standards.

## 1. God is the standard for parenting

*And, ye fathers, provoke not your children to wrath: but bring them up in the nurture and admonition of the Lord.* EPHESIANS 6:4.

As a Christian parent, your job is to bring up your children in the way of the Lord. You must use the word of God as your standard. You must not bring up your children in the way the world dictates, and don't follow the traditions of your people or the culture of your nation if they contradict God's way. Give your children Christian training.

## 2. Children are humans

*Fathers, provoke not your children to anger, lest they be discouraged.* COLOSSIANS 3:21.

Your children are human beings with needs and emotions. They get discouraged at some things, just like any adult does. You must avoid behaviour towards your children that embitters them or aggravates them. Do not demand of them more than they can bear. You will be held responsible if your children misbehave because you provoked them. Do not make yourself a source of temptation to your children. Don't make life difficult for them or they may rebel against your authority. Be realistic about what they are capable of.

## 3. Parenting gives direction to the child

*Train up a child in the way he should go: and when he is old, he will not depart from it.* PROVERBS 22:6.

As a parent, you must always ask yourself this question about the way you are training your children: which direction will they follow in future? Is your upbringing moving them in the right direction or wrong direction? You should be able to predict how they will turn out, based on how they are behaving now. If you feel they are going astray, then you need to change what you are doing. If you don't know what to do for the best, seek help now. It may be too late for the child if you leave it any longer.

## 4. Parenting without providing is unChristian

*But if any provide not for his own, and specially for those of his own house, he hath denied the faith, and is worse than an infidel.* 1 TIMOTHY 5:8.

According to this scripture, lack of provision for your children is a contradiction of your faith! Your salvation is in doubt if you don't provide for the needs of those who depend on you. Obviously, if there is a reason you can't work that is no fault of your own, then there are exceptions to this, but in general it is mandatory that parents meet the needs of their children – otherwise they are betraying the faith that they proclaim.

God is a provider and whoever claims to be associated with Him must be a provider too. If you claim to be a Christian and deny support to those who depend on you for survival, especially your children, then you have lied. You are not a Christian. You need to repent and recommit yourself to your family and the Lord.

## 5. Lack of discipline is a recipe for future disgrace

*The rod and reproof give wisdom: but a child left to himself bringeth his mother to shame.* PROVERBS 29:15.

If you fail to discipline your children you will deny them the opportunity to develop wisdom for living. Such children will grow up to be fools, not able to differentiate between good and evil. Due to their lack of wisdom they will be ignorant of the errors they are making. Don't avoid disciplining your children or you will be ashamed of them when they are older.

## 6. A well trained child brings peace of mind

*Correct thy son, and he shall give thee rest; yea, he shall give delight unto thy soul.* PROVERBS 29:17.

If you have invested energy in training your child, you will reap a harvest of peace tomorrow. If you thoroughly prepare your child for life, you won't be anxious about that child when he or she leaves home and has to make their own decisions. Instead, you will be delighted by their progress.

## 7. Negligence kills a child – not correction

*Withhold not correction from the child: for if thou beatest him with the rod, he shall not die.* PROVERBS 23:13.

A child who lacks a proper upbringing will soon die morally. If you don't correct and discipline your child because you don't want to inflict harmless pain upon your child, you will be inviting a much greater pain both to yourself and the child in the future. If you are too 'soft' on your children, you are letting them down.

## 8. Parenting must only be done in the Lord

*Children, obey your parents in the Lord: for this is right.* EPHESIANS 6:1.

Your children are to obey your teaching only if it complies with the way of the Lord. As a parent, you are to bring up your children in the Lord. You must not use any teaching or follow any doctrines that contradict the Bible. This implies that your children will be exonerated by God if they disobey your sinful instructions.

## 9. Respect matters

*Rebuke not an elder, but intreat him as a father; and the younger men as brethren; the elder women as mothers; the younger as sisters, with all purity.* 1 TIMOTHY 5:1-2.

You must teach your children to give other adults the same kind of respect that they owe to their parents. Teach your children to honour outsiders as if they were relatives. Respect matters.

## 10. Obedience to parents is mandatory

*My son, keep thy father's commandment, and forsake not the law of thy mother...* PROVERBS 6:20.

A child does not have an obligation to obey one of the parents, but not the other. Parents must ensure that their children obey both of them. This is the reason why parents must have a common front when dealing with their children. Don't undermine your wife or husband's authority by overruling them or disagreeing with their instructions in front of the children. Children must not notice disunity between their parents, otherwise they will take advantage of it. Children will naturally like the parent who is soft rather than the one that is harsh, so both parents must present the same levels of discipline.

## 11. Born foolish

*Foolishness is bound in the heart of a child; but the rod of correction shall drive it far from him.* PROVERBS 22:15.

A fool is a person who can't differentiate between good and evil. Every child was born foolish, in this sense, and so by nature they lack the understanding to make the right choices. It is proper parenting that replaces foolishness with wisdom. As a parent, never assume that your children will grow up to be wise if you have not planted wisdom them while they were young. A child that lacks a proper upbringing will grow up living by the foolishness that he or she was born with.

## 12. Born wicked

*The wicked are estranged from the womb: they go astray as soon as they be born, speaking lies.* PSALM 58:3.

All human beings are born with a tendency to sin – it is our inheritance from the very first couple, who fell from grace in the Garden of Eden. The proof of this is that you don't have to teach a child how to lie or disobey – they are quite able to do both without your help!

But there is also a genetic predisposition to certain kinds of bad behaviour that can be physically inherited from the previous generation. This is not yet fully understood, but some children are born with unhelpful traits, beyond what is considered normal, e.g. an addictive personality, where some people are more prone to addiction to drugs or alcohol.

Some children also inherit a spiritual evil from the parents or grandparents, or further back in the family line – perhaps a curse that runs in the family. Such evils can be broken in the name of Jesus, but as a parent you must be observant and be quick to act when you notice a certain strange behaviour in your children.

In some cases, a child may need deliverance before reaching adulthood, so as to expel the influence of certain demons from their lives. As a parent, watch out! But always ask your pastor before taking such important steps.

## 13. Born without glory

*As for Ephraim, their glory shall fly away like a bird, from the birth, and from the womb, and from the conception.* Hosea 9:11.

Due to curses, some children are born without glory. Such children are born in shame. A cursed mother or parent can't produce blessed children. Some ancestors have done so much evil that the wombs of their female descendants can't manifest glory. As a caring parent with your child's welfare always on your mind, if you notice certain physical abnormalities in your children you act quickly, seeking medical help and prayer. If you see a strange negative spiritual development in your children, you may need to seek spiritual assistance just as quickly.

## 14. Born sick

*And as Jesus passed by, he saw a man which was blind from his birth. And his disciples asked him, saying, Master, who did sin, this man, or his parents, that he was born blind? Jesus answered, Neither hath this man sinned, nor his parents: but that the works of God should be made manifest in him.* John 9:1-3.

These verses show that some children are born with medical complications or genetic defects. Children born with such conditions have done nothing wrong; they did not deserve their affliction.

For most parents it is natural to want to do everything you can to help such a child overcome their health condition, and to take care of them whatever disability or disease they may have. Only an irresponsible parent would abandon their child or fail to help them in every way possible. It is immoral to neglect such a child in his or her unfortunate situation.

When parents of a child born sick commit the situation into the hands of God, they can be sure of His comfort, strength and compassion. And God can bring glory to his name out of even the worst situations.

## 15. Parenting provides stability

*That we henceforth be no more children, tossed to and fro, and carried about with every wind of doctrine, by the sleight of men, and cunning craftiness, whereby they lie in wait to deceive...* EPHESIANS 4:14.

A child that does not receive a proper upbringing at home will be brought up by the society. And because different elements of society have different beliefs about life, the child will absorb a variety of conflicting influences and grow up morally confused – and so probably morally compromised.

The role of parents is to offer moral stability as well as physical care for their children. They must teach their children how to make the right decisions when faced with the diverse choices the world will bring to them. It is only the children who have been morally developed at home that will not be tossed to and fro by the deceptive doctrines of the world.

## 16. Parenting establishes the seriousness of discipline

*And ye have forgotten the exhortation which speaketh unto you as unto children, My son, despise not thou the chastening of the Lord, nor faint when thou art rebuked of him...* HEBREWS 12:5.

As a parent you must let your children know that your discipline, punishment and correction all has a serious purpose. It is not to make your life easier or theirs harder, it is to make them better people. Ensure your children take your discipline seriously. It is no laughing matter. You must never let your children undermine your discipline. They must not take your correction lightly or it will not change them.

Let your body language and tone of voice communicate the seriousness of your words. Let your children know that you are not joking when you correct them. Let them know the danger of not paying attention to your words and that there are consequences if they fail to obey.

## 17. Make the faith generational

*Tell ye your children of it, and let your children tell their children, and their children another generation.* JOEL 1:3.

Truth never changes. It endures time. As a parent, put your children in a position where they will be able to pass the training they are receiving from you on to their children when they grow up. How? By making your parenting strategy biblical.

Ensure your correction and discipline is Bible-based and explain that what you are doing is following what the Bible says. Point them to the verses and principles in the Bible that you are using. Help your children to imbibe biblical directives for their daily living by using the Bible as a mode of bringing up your children, and ensure that they understand it. If you just tell them what to do without explaining where your teaching comes from, they will not know how to find God's direction for their own children one day.

Remember, what you give to your children is what they will pass on to their own children when they grow up.

## 18. Practice impartation in parenting

*Then were there brought unto him little children, that he should put his hands on them, and pray: and the disciples rebuked them. But Jesus said, Suffer little children, and forbid them not, to come unto me: for of such is the kingdom of heaven. And he laid his hands on them...* MATTHEW 19:13-15.

Jesus laid His hands on children and prayed for them. He imparted spiritual blessings on them.

As a parent, you must occasionally lay your hands on your children and pray for them. Parenting is spiritual and you must approach it spiritually. Without the Holy Spirit's power, there is nothing a man can do to change a fellow human being, irrespective of age difference. But when you lay hands on your children and pray for them, you will be touching and empowering their spirits through the Holy Spirit. It is only when the inner person changes that the outer person will change.

## 19. Discipline must be consistent

*And ye shall teach them your children, speaking of them when thou sittest in thine house, and when thou walkest by the way, when thou liest down, and when thou risest up.* DEUTERONOMY 11:19.

The Bible teaches that passing on Christian teaching to your children must not be limited to certain locations like church services or meetings, or certain times like bedtime prayers or morning prayers. It is a 24/7 faith; it must be lived out all the time and can be taught anywhere.

It is the same with Christian parenting. You can't afford to 'switch off' and allow a lack of control when you don't feel up to it. As much as is possible, keep your children under control wherever you are. Don't only correct your children at home but also wherever you go outside the home. When your children misbehave publicly, correct them instantly but decently.

If they are among their peers, you don't have to embarrass them in front of their friends – instead, pull them to one side to tell them off. Show care for them at the same time as making it clear that you are consistent in your discipline.

And don't be influenced by parents with lower standards – don't allow your children to get away with something because they were not told off by the adults they were with at the time. Teach your children that if they know they are doing wrong, the fact that no one told them off at the time is no excuse.

Teach your children at home, outside the home, in the open, in secret, during the day, during the night, and in any location.

## 20. Parenting involves sharing testimonies

*Only take heed to thyself, and keep thy soul diligently, lest thou forget the things which thine eyes have seen, and lest they depart from thy heart all the days of thy life: but teach them thy sons, and thy sons' sons...* DEUTERONOMY 4:9.

God told the Israelites to teach their children about the miraculous works of God they had witnessed. This was to boost their faith in the living God. As a parent, share your testimonies with your children. Tell them how God has answered your prayers, delivered you from danger or given you wisdom to handle a situation. Tell them how God has met your needs and even granted the desires of your heart. Teach them how God has fought for you in life. Share the faithfulness of God with your children.

This will create confidence in the hearts of your children and it will help them to put their trust in God. Do not raise up a generation that will depart from God when they grow up.

## 21. Parenting involves equal treatment

*And in all the land were no women found so fair as the daughters of Job: and their father gave them inheritance among their brethren.* JOB 42:15.

This verse shows that Job did not discriminate between his daughters and sons – he gave all of them an inheritance. This was almost certainly breaking with the tradition of his own culture, in which only sons inherited wealth.

In parenting, both sons and daughters should be given the same treatment, discipline and gifts. There should be no favouritism. All children deserve the best training from their parents, irrespective of gender differences.

Obviously, there are some things that girls need to learn that boys don't, and vice versa, but apart from those natural differences, there should be no discrimination. Do not give better education to your sons at the expense of your daughters. That is evil in the eyes of God. Give your children equal access and opportunities, irrespective of their gender. Do not build one and destroy the other.

## 22. Parenting is about control

*A bishop then must be blameless... One that ruleth well his own house, having his children in subjection with all gravity.*
1 Timothy 3:2-4.

This verse shows that parenting is about control, about bringing children under your authority as a parent. This will involve an ability to influence the opinion, decisions and behaviour of a child. It means that the child must be willing to submit to the authority of the parents.

To be 'controlling' in our culture is seen as a modern sin – but that's because this secular kind of control arises through manipulation, threat and fear. Christian control, in contrast, arises through love. Love is the strongest weapon of control.

When a child is convinced that his or her parents genuinely love him or her, such a child is more likely to submit willingly to the authority of the parents. A child who enjoys care from a parent will not want to lose such care. Such a child will want to submit to the parents to keep enjoying the benefits of a good relationship with the parents. Unfortunately, control will become difficult if the child doubts the love of the parents.

## 23. Parenting is about diligence

*He that spareth his rod hateth his son: but he that loveth him chasteneth him betimes.* Proverbs 13:24.

Diligence means continual application of effort until the desired result is achieved. Parenting means that you continue to train or teach a child until you see the expected results.

'Betimes' in the verse above is old English for 'in good time' or 'speedily' – in other words, don't delay your discipline – don't let it slip. You must be diligent about it. The New American Standard Bible translation of this verse says: *"But he who loves him disciplines him diligently."*

For example, you are to continue telling your child to stop lying until he or she stops telling lies. You can't give up just because you get frustrated at having to repeat yourself again and again (though all parents know how annoying that is!). And timely discipline is part of being diligent as a parent. Never delay addressing an error you notice in your children – do it immediately, or you may forget, or the child may go and do the same thing again because you have not got round to addressing it the first time!

## 24. Parenting must keep the long-term goal in mind

*Chasten thy son while there is hope, and let not thy soul spare for his crying.* PROVERBS 19:18.

If you really care about your children, you will not avoid disciplining them. The phrase "let not thy soul spare for his crying" means that you must not let your sympathy for your son or daughter prevent you from disciplining them, even if they are weeping. Tears get to all parents, because we love our children and don't want to see them cry, but we are not truly loving them if we allow that emotion to prevent us from carrying out a reasonable punishment.

In fact, the New American Standard Bible translates this verse even more harshly for parents, because it says: *"Discipline your son while there is hope, and do not desire his death."* This does not mean that you literally want your child to die. It means that if you withhold punishment for some disobedience or other, you are condemning him to a future where he has not learned right from wrong. And if that happens, he may even end up abandoning the faith and receiving God's eternal punishment for his sin. So, in effect, failing to discipline a child is like condemning them to death!

You will not be judged by what you think towards your child, you will be judged by your actions towards your child. You may wish your child well in your heart but if you fail to discipline your child you are not taking care of your child. So, if you really wish your children a great future in life, discipline them. Keep the long-term goal in mind.

## 25. Share the importance of your teaching

*For the commandment is a lamp; and the law is light; and reproofs of instruction are the way of life...* PROVERBS 6:23.

Children need to be made aware of the reasons for your instructions, reprimands and punishments, as soon as they are old enough to understand.

Let your child know that your correction will lead that child down the right path in life. Do not just give instruction to your child, but educate the child about the significance of it. Your child is more likely to obey you if he or she understands that there are good reasons for obeying. If they know that disobedience will rob them of a good future and that obedience will bring good things into their lives, you are adding incentive to instruction, and wisdom for the future.

## 26. Parenting explains the importance of what company you keep

*He that walketh with wise men shall be wise: but a companion of fools shall be destroyed.* PROVERBS 13:20.

This verse shows what a child is likely to become by associating with wise people and foolish people. As a parent, you must educate your children about the possible consequences of association with different kinds of people, both positive and negative. Similarly, you must pay close attention to the kind of friends your children are making. Explain to your children why you want to discourage them from mixing with certain people.

## 27. Parenting is about fairness

*Even a child is known by his doings, whether his work be pure, and whether it be right.* PROVERBS 20:11.

This verse states that a child should be judged based on his or her actions. Do not judge your child based on what you assume or think the child has done or will do, or on what you believe the child thinks or feels, but judge only on what you are certain the child has actually done. It is unfair to treat children negatively based on your assumptions about their motivation for an action or your guess at who is responsible for something, because only God sees inside the mind and heart, and only He can see everything that happens.

## Seven

# THE SEED OF THE RIGHTEOUS

Your children are the seed of the righteous. You are the righteous by virtue of being a Christian; the righteousness of Jesus Christ has made you righteous. Therefore, every child that will come from you has an inheritance in the Lord. It is in the plan of God that after you have gone, He will continue with your children.

Therefore, your children are the future generation that God wants to continue with as His children. The eternal plan of God runs from generation to generation and your children form an integral part of that plan.

In this chapter, we will examine some things about your children that the Bible reveals are in the mind of God, and we shall turn them into prayer. If you can apply the following prayers to the lives of your children you will bring their lives into alignment with the purposes of God. Through the scriptures, you can see your children how God sees them and believe that their lives will turn out exactly as spelt out in the word of God.

## 1. The future of your children is secured in the Lord

*The children of thy servants shall continue, and their seed shall be established before thee.* PSALM 102:28.

Your children are the next generation that the Lord will continue with in His eternal plan for humanity. As God has been faithful to you, so He will be faithful to your children.

> **PRAYER**
> Almighty God, uphold my children in Yourself and let their lives bring You pleasure. Please establish my children in Your purposes and let them not depart from Your ways, in Jesus' name.

## 2. Your children are for signs and wonders

*Behold, I and the children whom the LORD hath given me are for signs and for wonders in Israel from the LORD of hosts, which dwelleth in mount Zion.* ISAIAH 8:18.

God wants to use your children to display His power to the world. As God has made your life an instrument for honour in His hands, so He wants to do the same with your children.

> **PRAYER**
> Father, let my children be instruments for honour in Your hands. Please keep my children from being used by the devil or man. Father, through my children, please expand Your kingdom, give hope to the hopeless, destroy the work of Satan and advance Your kingdom, in Jesus' name.

## 3. Your children shall never beg for food

*I have been young, and now am old; yet have I not seen the righteous forsaken, nor his seed begging bread.* PSALM 37:25.

The seed of the righteous shall never beg for food. The Lord will feed them always. He will take the shame of poverty far away from your children.

**PRAYER** *All-sufficient God, let my children always have good things in abundance. Let poverty be far away from my children and let them always be generous to others, in Jesus' name.*

## 4. Your children shall dwell in salvation

*Though hand join in hand, the wicked shall not be unpunished: but the seed of the righteous shall be delivered.* PROVERBS 11:21.

God will not let enemies prevail over your children. He will personally take charge of the deliverance of your children from any form of captivity of the enemy.

**PRAYER** *Father, You are my deliverer. Please be the deliverer of my children through all their days. Arise against the enemies of my children. Never let enemies prevail over my children. Keep my children in Your salvation always, in Jesus' name.*

## 5. Your children shall be stronger than their enemies

*That in blessing I will bless thee, and in multiplying I will multiply thy seed as the stars of the heaven, and as the sand which is upon the sea shore; and thy seed shall possess the gate of his enemies...* GENESIS 22:17.

The seed of the righteous shall possess the gates of their enemies. That means they will exercise dominion over their enemies. Your children shall always be ahead of their enemies, and will rule over them. Whoever rises against your children shall be brought low before them.

**PRAYER** *Father, multiply your blessings on my children spiritually, physically, mentally, financially and materially. Make my children too strong for their enemies. Make my children defeat their enemies in all their days, in Jesus' name.*

## 6. Your children shall be mighty and blessed

*His seed shall be mighty upon earth: the generation of the upright shall be blessed.* PSALM 112:2.

God will not let your children be weak. He will spiritually empower them to be strong. His blessings shall rest upon their lives.

> PRAYER: Father, make my children mighty and let Your divine blessings rest upon them all their lives. Please release Your generational blessing into my lineage, in Jesus' name.

## 7. Your children shall never lack security

*In the fear of the LORD is strong confidence: and his children shall have a place of refuge.* PROVERBS 14:26.

Your children will always have God as their refuge. They shall not lack security. The Lord will hide them in Himself.

> PRAYER: Father, You have been my refuge. Please be my children's refuge for as long as they live. Hide my children in Yourself. Let no evil find my children, in Jesus' name.

## 8. Your children are children of covenant

*And I will establish my covenant between me and thee and thy seed after thee in their generations for an everlasting covenant, to be a God unto thee, and to thy seed after thee.* GENESIS 17:7.

Your children will enjoy the blessings of the covenant God made with Abraham. They shall be co-heirs with you in the covenant of God. As you have enjoyed a covenant relationship with God, so your children will too.

> PRAYER: Father, please be a God to my children in all their days. Let the Abrahamic covenant work for my children. Please walk with my children always, in Jesus' name.

## 9. Your children have been divinely chosen by God

Only the LORD had a delight in thy fathers to love them, and he chose their seed after them, even you above all people, as it is this day. Deuteronomy 10:15.

Your children are chosen by God. They are destined for good things. The favour of God is on them. Your children have the goodness of God on them. They have God's grace over their lives.

> **PRAYER**
> *Father, I thank You because You have chosen my children for Your goodness even before they were born. Please let my children live above the limitations of life in all their ways. Please don't let what limited me in life limit my children in their own lives, in Jesus' name.*

## 10. Your children shall be unlimited in blessings

*And the angel of the LORD said unto her, I will multiply thy seed exceedingly, that it shall not be numbered for multitude.*
Genesis 16:10.

God told Sarah that He would make her descendants an uncountable multitude, as she was under the covenant God had made with Abraham to make a nation from his family. As we are in Christ, we receive all the spiritual blessings of the covenant God has made with us through Christ's blood, shed for us. Ephesians 1:3 says that God "hath blessed us with all spiritual blessings in heavenly places in Christ".

Your children's fruitfulness shall have no boundary. God wants to bless your children without any limitation.

> **PRAYER**
> *Unlimited Father, please make my children unlimited in life and let Your blessings flow into their lives unceasingly. Father, flatten every demonic boundary the enemy wants to build around my children, in Jesus' name.*

## 11. Your children shall become a blessing to the nations

*And thy seed shall be as the dust of the earth, and thou shalt spread abroad to the west, and to the east, and to the north, and to the south: and in thee and in thy seed shall all the families of the earth be blessed.* GENESIS 28:14.

This verse prophesies that the seed of Abraham would become a source of blessing to the nations. As Christians are now included in Abraham's children (we are grafted into the tree of Israel – see ROMANS 11:16-17), we are also the distributors of divine blessings and so are our children. Your children shall be so blessed that through them, God will begin to bless other people near to them and far away.

**PRAYER**: Father, turn my children into distributors of Your blessings. Please make my children become sources of Your blessings. Through my children, let poverty and lack be terminated in the lives of people, in Jesus' name.

## 12. Your children will always enjoy God's mercy

*I will be his father, and he shall be my son. If he commit iniquity, I will chasten him with the rod of men, and with the stripes of the children of men: But my mercy shall not depart away from him, as I took it from Saul, whom I put away before thee.* 2 SAMUEL 7:14-15.

Your children will enjoy divine mercy. God promised through Samuel that His mercy would not depart from King David, and we are in King David's line since Jesus was in David's line and we are now joint-heirs or co-heirs with Christ (ROMANS 8:17). Therefore God will never withdraw His mercy from us and our children. The care of God for your children is guaranteed. God will always be gracious and merciful to them.

> **PRAYER** Merciful Father, please let your goodness and mercy follow my children all their days of their lives. Your grace will sustain them wherever they go, in Jesus' name.

## 13. The Spirit of the Lord shall always rest upon your children

*For I will pour water upon him that is thirsty, and floods upon the dry ground: I will pour my spirit upon thy seed, and my blessing upon thine offspring…* ISAIAH 44:3.

The seed of the righteous shall be Spirit-filled. The Lord will pour His Spirit upon your children so that they can know Him and be used by Him. The Spirit of the Lord shall take control of the life of your children. They shall always be led of God.

> **PRAYER** Father, may your Spirit fill and lead my children and enable them to always walk in your wisdom and guidance. Please reign in the decision-making of my children and take charge of their choices in all situations, in Jesus' name.

## 14. Your children shall be restorers of ruins

*For thou shalt break forth on the right hand and on the left; and thy seed shall inherit the Gentiles, and make the desolate cities to be inhabited.* ISAIAH 54:3.

The seed of the righteous will rebuild the ruins. They will restore what the enemy has destroyed. They shall be a restorer of lost glory. Your children shall bring life in places where there was desolation.

> **PRAYER** Prayer: Father, use my children to restore lost blessings. Through my children, bring total restoration to lives. Please make my children Your battle-axe to destroy the work of Satan in the lives of people, in Jesus' name.

## 15. Your children will bring glory to God

*And their seed shall be known among the Gentiles, and their offspring among the people: all that see them shall acknowledge them, that they are the seed which the LORD hath blessed.* Isaiah 61:9.

The seed of the righteous shall be used by God to advertise His glory to the world. Those who see your children will see that they have been blessed by God, and give Him the glory. The Lord will use the lives of your children to spread His name in the world.

PRAYER: Father, let Your glory rest upon my children always. Please decorate the lives of my children with blessings that can't be hidden. Let the world confess that my children are blessed by the Lord.

## 16. Your children shall be un-removable

*For as the new heavens and the new earth, which I will make, shall remain before me, saith the LORD, so shall your seed and your name remain.* Isaiah 66:22.

The seed of the righteous shall not be cast away. They shall not be removed. They will remain where God has planted them. No power will be able to uproot your children where God has placed them.

PRAYER: Father, sustain my children in their places where you establish them. Let no power be able to uproot them where you have planted them. Make my children un-removable, in Jesus' name.

## 17. Your children shall be taught by the Lord

*And all thy children shall be taught of the LORD; and great shall be the peace of thy children.* Isaiah 54:13.

The seed of the righteous shall be taught of the Lord. The Lord will lead your children in the path of life. They will enjoy divine guidance throughout their life.

**PRAYER** Prayer: Father, teach my children the way to live, every day of their lives. Please keep them in Your guidance always and let Your peace never depart from them, in Jesus' name.

## 18. Your children shall have a reward for their labour

*They shall not labour in vain, nor bring forth for trouble; for they are the seed of the blessed of the LORD, and their offspring with them.* ISAIAH 65:23.

This verse indicates that the works of your children's hands will be blessed. Whatever they put their hand to shall prosper. They will never experience fruitless effort.

**PRAYER** Father, may my children's work always be profitable. Take failure and fruitless effort far away from their lives. Please let them be successful and have the reward for their labours, in Jesus' name.

## 19. Your children shall command blessings on earth

*His soul shall dwell at ease; and his seed shall inherit the earth.* PSALM 25:13.

This psalm indicates that your children will receive and enjoy every earthly and spiritual blessing that is in their best interest, here on earth. They will not lack any blessing that they need to live a glorious life.

**PRAYER** Father, let the riches and wealth in secret places be uncovered by my children. Let both Your earthly and spiritual blessings be upon them all their days, in Jesus' name.

## 20. Your children are co-heirs with Christ

*For the promise is unto you, and to your children, and to all that are afar off, even as many as the Lord our God shall call.* ACTS 2:39.

As you have received the Holy Spirit, so will your children. As you have enjoyed the grace of God, so will your children. As God has shown you pardon, so He will pardon your children. All the promises of God are for both you and your children.

**PRAYER**

*Father, let Your promises be fulfilled for my children. Let my children enjoy the benefits of Your promises all their lives. Please perform Your word in the lives of all my children, in Jesus' name.*

# BOOKS FROM THE SAME AUTHOR

Journey to the Next Level

The New Creature

Building a Glorious Home:
*A Pathway to a Successful Marriage*

The Winning Formula

The Enemy of Marriage

The Word that Heals

Faith That Always Wins:
*Discover The Power Of A Living Faith*

This book, and all other books from the same author, are available at Christian bookstores and distributors worldwide.

They can also be obtained through online retail partners such as Amazon or by contacting the author on the address below.

**Contacts:**
21-23 Stokescroft, Bristol, BS1 3PY
United Kingdom

**E-mail:**
kkasali@yahoo.com

**Telephone:**
+44 (0)7727159581

www.ingramcontent.com/pod-product-compliance
Lightning Source LLC
Chambersburg PA
CBHW070546300426
**44113CB00011B/1808**